Awakening to God's Voice

A 90-DAY JOURNEY FROM HIS HEART TO YOURS

CONSTANCE BROCATO AND NIKI KRAUSS

HOUSEBOAT
PUBLISHING

Cover and interior layout by Typewriter Creative Co.
Cover illustrations by Mariah Danielle at CreativeMarket.com
Interior artwork by Melissa Weiss
Author photos by Tammy Cromer

Unless otherwise noted, all Scripture quotations are taken from the Holy Bible, English Standard Version (ESV), Crossway, a publishing ministry of Good News Publishers, Wheaton, Illinois, © 2001, 2016. Used by permission. All rights reserved.

Scripture quotations marked (NLT) are taken from the Holy Bible, New Living Translation, used by permission of Tyndale House Publishers, Inc., Carol Stream, Illinois 60188, © 1996, 2004, 2015. All rights reserved.

Scripture quotations marked The Message are taken from The Message: The Bible in Contemporary Language, translated by Eugene H. Peterson, © 1993, 2002, 2018, used by permission of NavPress, Inc., represented by Tyndale House Publishers, Inc. All rights reserved.

ISBN 979-8-9903396-1-3(Paperback)
ISBN 979-8-9903396-2-0 (Hardcover)
ISBN 979-8-9903396-3-7 (Jacketed Hardcover)
ISBN 979-8-9903396-0-6 (eBook)

Also by Niki Krauss

Little Girl Mended: A Memoir

To Jesus, Our Lord and Savior . . .

May Your name be honored, glorified, and praised

Introduction

WHILE CELEBRATING OUR BIRTHDAYS TOGETHER on a rented houseboat, we felt inspired by the beauty of the lake and the joyful experience we shared. We decided then and there to write a book together as we had so often dreamed to do. We wondered, *What if we took a Bible passage and each wrote separately about the same verse and what it means to us—what we hear from God in it?*

One of the ways God speaks to us is through Scripture. *Awakening to God's Voice* focuses on the individualized aspect the Spirit uses to speak from His Word to us. You may hear something completely different from Him than we do, even though we're all reading the same passage.

Awakening to God's Voice offers two distinct reflections on each verse to read back to back in the same day, along with relevant personal stories from both of us to help you reflect on God's voice in your own story. Each day's devotions conclude with a short prayer, encouraging a longer conversation with the Lord. You'll find no chronological order to our devotions or our stories. We wrote as we heard from God, randomly and as He decided to speak.

Our hope is that you will be immersed and deeply impacted during your reflective times alone with God. We pray you, our dear reader, will become more available and attuned to hearing God speak from His heart to yours. May you experience in reading what we experienced in writing—the wonder and awe of awakening to God's voice through His Word.

—Constance & Niki

Day 1

Stampeding Goats!

CONSTANCE

TWICE A YEAR, I'M DRAWN to the mountains of North Carolina, my Eden for rest and reflection. The majestic Smoky Mountains capture my attention, the beautiful floral displays light my heart, and long nature walks entice my body to napping and a glass of wine. As I traverse the hills and valleys, strolling along streams and ponds, I am lured into the woods. The trails jealously grab for my attention as I walk in solitude with God.

One morning I stopped to gaze on a herd of goats in an open yard with a vacant building as the backdrop. I tried to woo the goats closer for a picture, but they weren't interested. Anticipating the forest trail ahead, I picked up a long branch for a walking stick. Lifting my stick, I noticed the herd stampeding toward me. The sight was exhilarating yet startling! An electric fence between me and the approaching goats offered me comfort and safety. I was shocked at how quickly they abandoned chewing and roaming to run full speed toward me when I picked up a stick.

When the goats saw the staff in my hand, it was their cue to come to me. The shepherd's staff, a long and slender stick, conveys authority, power, and discipline. It also provides protection, care, love, and guidance, indicative of a familiar shepherd. Goats are herd animals by nature, they desire to be near those who care for them. They reciprocate by remaining close, touching, and even sidling up to humans and other animals. They must enjoy being adored. Don't we all? Jesus enjoys our adoration! He is the Good Shepherd, and His sheep (and goats) know His voice.

The passage in Psalm 23 affirms David's view of the Lord as a Shepherd, who leads us, cares for our well-being, and provides goodness and mercy for those who follow Him. The beauty of the Shepherd and His sheep is in comfort and protection. ". . . for you are with me; your rod and your staff, they comfort me, and I shall dwell in the house of the Lord forever" (Psalm 23:6c). Is the Lord your Shepherd? Are you enjoying His nearness and protection today?

Shadows

NIKI

RECENTLY, WHILE ON A CRUISE with my family, I watched my nine-year-old granddaughter shadowbox with her Great Aunt Mae and Uncle Jim in the bright sunshine on the top deck of the ship. They weren't throwing punches, but Charlotte was trying her best to step on their shadows as they darted away, always seeming to be one step ahead of her. With shrieks of laughter, they ran around in circles. It was fun entertainment because, unlike real boxing, everyone knows a shadow can't hurt you.

Such it is with "the shadow of death." Because of Christ's death and resurrection, only the shadow of death remains. We who have submitted our hearts and lives to Jesus pass through death and into an eternity in the presence of God. Death has lost its terror. It's what brings us, at last, face to face with our Savior.

As I'm in the latter years of my life, I treasure that truth. Leaving this life is not the end but the beginning. This life is but a vapor, temporary like the shadow. James gives a rich picture of the transiency of life, "—yet you do not know what tomorrow will bring. What is your life? For you are a mist that appears for a little time and then vanishes" (James 4:14). We've all watched our breath on a frigid day, it appears as vapor and quickly fades away. In light of eternity, that's our earthly lives. Life is temporary, and death is the gateway to paradise for those who love the Lord with their whole hearts, minds, and spirits.

I've heard people say they fear death because it's something everyone has to do alone. But we don't pass through the valley of the shadow of death alone. We don't do anything alone; Jesus will never leave or abandon us. He changes everything—even death.

Glorious Father, You are the One who leads me, loves me, and walks with me. I am guided by your rod and staff. I long to see You face to face, to be in Your presence forever. Amen.

Day 2

Jesus wept.

—John 11:35

Tears Matter to Jesus

NIKI

EIGHTEEN MONTHS AFTER OUR YOUNGEST son was married, his wife's grandfather unexpectedly passed away. Popo was a wise man, loved and respected by many, including my son who spent many hours in thoughtful conversation with him. My husband, Joe, and I flew from Virginia to Dallas to attend Popo's funeral, because we loved and respected him but also because we wanted to be present to support our son, daughter-in-law, and her family through a difficult time.

At the cemetery, after the service, my son turned, saw me, and came weeping into my arms. I held him close and wept with him. There's something moving and oh so hard about seeing a grown man weep. I wept too because my heart ached over the pain and grief he was suffering. I shared in his pain because I loved Popo but also because I deeply love my son, and his pain is always my pain.

Jesus is God, but He was also human, having all of the human emotions we have. He wept at the sight of Martha and Mary weeping over the death of their brother. He had compassion for them in their grief and pain, and He still has compassion for us today in our suffering. As God, and as Man, He knows what we're feeling, and He cares deeply.

Why would Martha and Mary's suffering cause Jesus to weep, though, when He knew He would turn their mourning into rejoicing with Lazarus' resurrection? He felt compassion, yes, but He was also witnessing the heinous consequences of sin. Sin brought death into the world, and Jesus knew the pain sin and death brought for mankind.

Jesus also knew He was bringing Lazarus back from glorious heaven to the cursed world where he would have to suffer death a second time. Jesus knew heaven like we can't know it because He was there before His incarnation. Perhaps He was grieved to remove Lazarus from paradise and God's presence. But Jesus was always about following the Father's will. Though it may have grieved Him to the point of weeping, Jesus knew bringing Lazarus back from the dead was necessary for the faith of those watching and to bring glory to the Father.

Likely Jesus wept with compassion for Martha and Mary, He wept in anger over sin's consequences, and He wept in sorrow for removing Lazarus from God's presence. God cares about our suffering, our sin, and our relationship with Him. Just as I held my son in his suffering, Jesus wraps His arms of comfort around us in our suffering. He weeps for us and with us. He cares deeply when we wander into sin, and He is always ready to draw near to us when we turn back to Him in repentance.

Holy Suffering

CONSTANCE

A CLOSE FRIEND SHARED A DIFFICULT and painful event in her life. Because I love her and the depth of our relationship, I'm profoundly pulled into her pain as if it were mine. My compassion for her connects with her suffering. At some level, I'm angry because the pain was initiated by another person, and I desire retribution. In another way, compassion leads me to empathy and interceding for her to allow God to bring judgment.

I imagine Jesus experienced intense emotions when He learned of His cousin John's beheading. Scripture details the events around John the Baptist's death in Matthew 14. The daughter of Herodias, Herod's brother's wife, danced for Herod at his birthday party. It pleased Herod so much he made an oath to give her whatever she would ask. Herodias prompted her daughter to request John's head on a platter. And so it was. This appalling act was despicable and heinous. Absolute anger for retribution would be expected, but Jesus, deeply grieved, withdrew in a boat to a desolate place by Himself, most likely to be alone with His Father.

Pain and joy are often companions in our lives. The emotional ups and downs, the struggles and victories, the injustices and freedoms strike at various times. Jesus knew it well, especially when he lost his cousin and friend. Surrounded by suffering, Jesus often healed the sick, lame, and blind; delivered those under demonic oppression; and befriended the outsider. He witnessed the pain of others and had compassion, bringing life and joy into their lives.

There was no retribution for the pain Jesus endured at His own crucifixion, but God had a glorious plan of resurrection for Him and for us. "Vengeance is mine . . . . For the Lord will vindicate his people and have compassion on his servants" (Deuteronomy 32:35–36a).

God of Glory, though there is pain, there is also joy. You are close and You care for me in every circumstance. May I be connected to Your heart of compassion for those who need a Redeemer. Help me to submit all things to You. Amen.

Day 3

We love because he first loved us.

—1 John 4:19

Love Is Hardwired in Us

CONSTANCE

THE DAY OUR SON, SEBASTIAN, was born was one of the greatest days of our lives. This bundle of sweetness was ours, and we were mesmerized by the depth of love we felt for him. My husband, Woody, and I had dreams for this little one; we would protect and love him no matter what. Where did this capacity to love so intensely come from? One tiny babe was changing our lives moment by moment.

Our love connection began in the womb and exponentially grew after birth, as Sebastian and I gazed upon each other. The gaze between us was love, the formation of trust, and the building of a beautiful relationship. When a baby doesn't experience love in the early years, it can lead to poor brain development, low self-esteem, and failure to thrive. Love is vital—as crucial between a mom and a baby as it is between one with another. We all have a need for love. That need is hardwired in us by a benevolent God who desires a love relationship with us, His children. Remember, God, who knew us while we were in the womb, first loved us!

If humans can feel this powerful love with one another, can you imagine the Source of love extending His love to us? The gaze between God and His children becomes so powerful we long for more. The yearning of our heart for Him envelops us, and a relationship forms that draws us deeper into that wonderful mystery of love.

God won't force us, but He invites us to love Him. We can choose His love by accepting the gift of salvation through Jesus and cultivating the relationship by abiding in His Word, learning to be quiet with Him, and listening for His voice.

Let Him love you extravagantly as you walk in the world with love. Love moves us, love changes us, and love wins.

Mommy's Love

NIKI

FROM THE TIME MY TWO BOYS were born, I told each of them, "Nobody loves you like your mommy loves you." I'd say it snuggling on the sofa, when tucking them in at night, or at any time, really. I remember their dad saying, "What about me? I'm their dad, and I love them, too." I knew he loved them but not the way I did.

What I didn't understand then was that God could have said the same thing to me. No matter how much I love my kids, God loves them more. But in those years of young motherhood, my thinking didn't include God very often. There were many years when we didn't go to church at all. It's one of my greatest regrets as a mom. We didn't give our kids the spiritual upbringing we were charged to give them. "You shall therefore lay up these words of mine in your heart and in your soul . . . . You shall teach them to your children, talking of them when you are sitting in your house, and when you are walking by the way, and when you lie down, and when you rise" (Deuteronomy 11:18–19). None of that happened in our house. How I wish we had taught them about how much God loves them. But in raising children, there are no do-overs.

Yet God pursues us despite our mistakes. Our youngest son came to know the Lord through no help from me or his father. In fact, it was seeing his love for Jesus and his growing faith when he was in his twenties that brought me to seek a relationship with God for myself. It took another decade for me to understand that Jesus wants my all. Coming to the point of full surrender—God's will, God's way in everything—finally brought the heart change I didn't even know I needed. The Holy Spirit did the rest.

Our oldest son is a different story. He believes Jesus lived, but he doesn't believe Jesus makes a difference in our eternity. He also has no idea of the abundant life Jesus promises and of which he's missing out. A relationship with the Lord changes everything. Maybe that's what he's afraid of. But nothing in this world is better than life with Jesus. If my son only knew what he was missing!

Benevolent Father, the One who loves my soul, show me how to love You and others the way You love me. Thank You for the greatest gift of Your Son and for the Holy Spirit. Amen.

Day 4

For as in Adam all die, so also in Christ shall all be made
alive . . . . The last enemy to be destroyed is death.

—1 Corinthians 15:22, 26

Of Promises and Butterflies

NIKI

I ONCE BOUGHT BUTTERFLY KITS for my three grandkids. I bought one for myself, as well, so we could share the experience while living long distance from one another. We each received a habitat with a small food source and five tiny caterpillars. After traveling through the mail system, they all looked dead. But we followed the instructions, hoping we would see signs of life. Within a couple of days in the right environment, squiggly movement began in each of our habitats. One of my grandson's was indeed dead, but nineteen caterpillars seemed to rise from the grave.

The bedrock of Christianity is Christ's resurrection. Sin brought death into the world, and Christ's resurrection brought eternal life. Without resurrection, there would be no hope of eternity. And Jesus promised all will rise from the dead. "Do not marvel at this, for an hour is coming when all who are in the tombs will hear his voice and come out" (John 5:28–29a). The resurrection of the dead is assured.

Christ's final judgment of evil will cast Satan (and death) into the lake of fire for all eternity. And what of us who belong to Jesus? When we're resurrected, we'll be given new bodies, a new heaven, and a new earth where God will dwell with us forever. I sometimes wonder what my new body will look like. Will it even be a body as we know it? I imagine it to be the perfection God intended from the beginning.

My grandkids and I watched our caterpillars every day as they crawled around the habitats. Within two weeks, they all had made their way to the top and attached themselves to the lid in chrysalises. In a couple more weeks, beautiful butterflies emerged—all nineteen. We filmed ourselves opening the lids and watching them flutter away, sharing the videos with one another. It was something special.

From squirming little caterpillars came beauty. That's how I imagine my new body will be—made to perfection, all through Jesus who makes what was once dead, alive.

In the Silence

CONSTANCE

IN AUGUST 2023, A MEMORIAL service was held in New York City for pastor and author, Tim Keller. I watched online as friends and family told humorous but heartfelt stories about their loved one. David, one of Tim's three sons, approached the podium to speak, but he couldn't. The silence was deep and full, powerfully intense, as we labored with David together in his grief. Supported by his mom and brother on each side, David began to pray, slowly and with emotion. Then, he spoke of his father, who was bigger than his years, wiser and kinder than most, and passionately loved God.

God's presence in those quiet moments created a sense of awe. The silence was full of grief and hope shared among a community in their sadness and longing for life to be without death. Our grief is real, but our hope in the resurrection is firm. Grief is a time of remembering and lamenting as we process our loved one's passing. It's a time to lean into the Holy Spirit, our Comforter.

Death has been the enemy of God's children since the Garden of Eden, but one day, it won't be so. Martha's sadness at her brother's illness turned to grief when Lazarus died. Jesus arrived days later to find a grieving village of family and friends and was moved by their sadness. Jesus said to Martha, "I am the resurrection and the life. Whoever believes in me, though he die, yet shall he live, and everyone who lives and believes in me shall never die. Do you believe this?" (John 11:25–26). Jesus, in His own grief, shows them something about the Kingdom of God by performing a resurrection miracle. Jesus called Lazarus to come out of the tomb, and he did! This miracle was the last one mentioned in John's Gospel prior to Jesus' own death and resurrection. What a wonderful day it was!

We grieve, but as believers in Christ, we grieve not like those who have no hope for eternity with God (1 Thessalonians 4:13).

Beloved Father, You grieve with me and You comfort me. Lord, I need Your presence every day. Thank You for the promise of eternal life in a new body tailormade for me. I cherish Your every promise. Amen.

Day 5

"Is not this the carpenter, the son of Mary and brother of James and Joses and Judas and Simon? And are not his sisters here with us?" And they took offense at him. And Jesus said to them, "A prophet is not without honor except in his hometown and among his relatives and in his own household."

—Mark 6:3–4

Differences That Don't Divide

CONSTANCE

IN A REFLECTIVE MOMENT WITH our Scripture verse, I saw a truth I hadn't previously considered. The Holy Family was a blended family, just like mine. Jesus had a stepfather, Joseph, and half brothers and sisters. I reckon things were not so smooth between Him and His siblings at times. Jesus was conceived by the Holy Spirit and born of the virgin Mary, making Him very different. And being different often brings jealousy and tension. In fact, the Bible highlights the stories of many dysfunctional families.

Disagreements, battles, logistical movements of families, and tribes intermarrying all caused division in ancient times. We can find similar divisions in our own families, but I believe we can also create a better humanity, one family at a time, and usher in a taste of heaven to earth. A changed humanity would have a willingness to forge commitments for cohesive family units and begs for restructuring tools, including better communication skills, implementing new traditions for the family, and exploring different activities that can be done together. Sometimes a therapist can help a blended family through a difficult transition.

According to my internet search, forty percent of families in the United States are blended, and seventy percent of blended families end in divorce. My blended family has come a long way from thirty-three years ago. We now welcome each other's uniqueness and realize we all want the same things—acceptance, respect, commitment, and love. We aren't perfect, but our intentions are right.

We're all God's sons and daughters, thus brothers and sisters. But this truth gets muddled within our own families and in the world. What a beautiful mosaic we could create if we were willing to step into a more unified human community, including our blended families. Our individual differences and unique qualities wouldn't divide us. Our words would be kinder. Our political and religious affiliations would be a source of enlightenment and healthy communication. We need God *and* each other. "For you are all one in Christ Jesus" (Galatians 3:28b). Is there some small step we each can take to help create unity in the world?

Family Can Be Hard

NIKI

WHEN I FIRST BEGAN TO READ the Bible as a newlywed at age twenty-one, I was astounded at how wrong I had been about what following Jesus meant and looked like. I had been completely wrapped up in obeying the man-made rules of the denomination in which I was raised. Delving into what God has to say in Scripture changed the very essence of what I believed about Him. I wanted others, especially my family, to know what I had discovered.

On our first trip back to my hometown, Joe and I attempted to tell my parents we were going to follow what God said in the Bible and not what men said about God. We wanted them to see how misguided we all had been. That's not exactly the way the conversation went. They closed their ears to anything we tried to say and told us they didn't want to hear such blasphemy. I wound up in tears, sobbing into a pillow in my old bedroom.

Jesus gave us the mission of telling the world about Him. But how often do we remain silent because we're afraid of the reaction someone may have, or we're afraid of rejection? Jesus warned us of rejection. "The one who hears you hears me, and the one who rejects you rejects me, and the one who rejects me rejects him who sent me" (Luke 10:16). Our responsibility is to share Jesus with the world. The reaction to our telling about what Jesus has done for us is God's responsibility. We can't change anyone's heart. That's the job of the Holy Spirit.

Our own loved ones can be the hardest people to whom we'll have the opportunity to witness. This I know to be true. Jesus knew it, too, in Nazareth. But we still have to be ready to take the opportunity and entrust the outcome to the Lord.

My parents and I never talked about faith again. When you've tried and been rejected, you realize the words may need to come from someone else. But there is something we can always do. We can keep praying.

Heavenly Father, please make Yourself known to the ones I love in a way that changes everything for them. Draw them to You and open their eyes to see You for who You truly are and to see their need for a Savior. Whatever and whomever it takes, Lord. Amen.

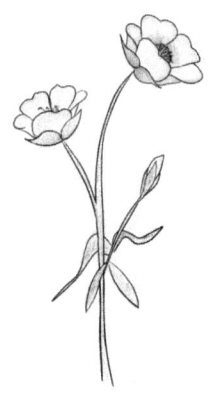

Day 6

"For as the heavens are higher than the earth, so are my ways higher than your ways and my thoughts than your thoughts."

—*Isaiah 55:9*

Tangled Threads

NIKI

MANY DECADES AGO, I WAS into needlepoint and counted cross-stitch. One year, while Joe was deployed, I made Christmas stockings for us. It was a long project but satisfying in the end. Have you ever looked at the back of a needlepoint or tapestry though? Tangled threads and countless knots are everywhere. It looks like how you'd picture chaos. The back of a needlecraft project is like the side of life we get to experience. With our limited vision and understanding, we become stuck on the reverse side, in chaos, making it difficult to see the beautiful picture God is creating on the front side.

Isaiah 55:9 can either bring great comfort or great frustration. It depends on perspective. Have you ever thought to yourself, *If only God would show me what He's doing, then I could trust Him more?* But faith is believing when we can't see the answer.

Desiring to know God's ways isn't anything new. In Exodus 33:13, Moses asked God to show him His ways, "Now therefore, if I have found favor in your sight, please show me now your ways, that I may know you . . . ." Like Moses, when we're in the middle of the chaos, we begin to put our trust in the idea that if God shared His plan with us, we would then have deeper faith. If we only knew, we would have peace. We still want to be all-knowing, just like Eve in Eden when tempted by Satan to eat from the tree of the knowledge of good and evil.

But God's desire is that we seek to *know Him,* not what's going to happen next. God's response to Moses' request was to promise His presence and rest instead. We can trust God is with us in our circumstances, no matter how much or how little we understand. Growing, maturing faith is trusting in God's goodness even when our circumstances say otherwise. It's not for us to question why. May our faith allow us to say instead, "Not my will, Lord, but Your will be done."

No matter how tangled and chaotic life may feel, God has purpose in it. May we fully trust in His goodness, even when we don't understand.

Awkward Moments!

CONSTANCE

AFTER SEEING MY DOCTOR, I STOPPED at the front desk to schedule a future appointment. I noticed the receptionist's face and said, "I love your face." Suddenly, I felt a bit uncomfortable since she didn't take her eyes from her computer. But I jumped back in, "Your lips and face remind me of my cousin, Sue." Still, nothing. Now, I'm feeling awkward. I love to engage people in conversation, but this time, I was recalling when Sue said, "Constance, sometimes you should just keep your mouth shut!" Then, it happened. The receptionist gave me my next appointment date—August 23, Sue's birthday! Well, that got her attention for the first time during this humiliating engagement.

Baffled by this strangeness, finally full of smiles and ready to engage in conversation, we became more than strangers.

This experience had me thinking of the encounters Jesus had. The man at the pool of Bethesda, an invalid from youth and resigned to his condition of thirty-eight years, found himself face to face with Jesus. Or the awkward time when Jesus took saliva mixed with clay, put it on the eyes of a blind man, and he was healed. Surely, these moments were awkward for these men and other bystanders. But they heard Jesus' words, responded, and were delivered (John 5:1–9, John 9).

Jesus provoked people with His words on many occasions. The sullen hearts of those whom Christ encountered often turned to hearts of joy—hope restored, bodies healed, and sins forgiven. Awkward conversations turned to miracles. It was far more difficult for the religious leaders to allow their hearts to be swayed by the Spirit of God. They were resistant and missed who was right in front of them.

My time with the receptionist wasn't a holy moment, but it was unique and, ultimately, caught her attention. Why I said what I said to her, I can't say. I'm confident, however, neither of us will forget our encounter.

I'm intrigued by God's creativity in how He arranges "settings" for engagement with others. I love the "open doors" for sharing our faith in Jesus. Find someone today with whom you can share your faith or just enjoy a conversation. God's ways may surprise you.

Blessed Father, place me where You want to use me for Your purposes. You are only and always good. May Your words bring me the peace, rest, and comfort of Your presence. Amen.

Day 7

Then he said to them, "Why are you afraid?
Do you still have no faith?"

—*Mark 4:40*

In the Boat With a Lifesaver

CONSTANCE

FEAR IS NOT MY FRIEND WHEN I'm in the deep end of a pool or out too far in the ocean. I'm not a good swimmer. I can boogie board, swim with fins, snorkel for hours, or go across a pool. These are my limits. I can't even imagine being cast into the ocean in a raging storm without a lifeboat! I can't say for sure, but fear and panic might just snuff out my faith.

I love the story behind these words in Mark 4:40. The disciples are weathering a raging storm with rolling high seas in a not-so-large boat, and Jesus is sound asleep. How is it possible Jesus is sleeping? He was exhausted, most likely, and trusted the disciples had learned a little bit about faith and fear.

Why were the disciples afraid? They were with Jesus when he performed numerous miracles. They had experienced the impossible. Did they not remember the power of God in Jesus?

The disciples frantically awoke Jesus, and He rebuked them. What did Jesus know that the others didn't? Jesus often used questions, even questions as answers, when speaking to people. As in this case, He wanted them to formulate their own answers from deep within their hearts—to think about their fear or inability to take charge and speak to the raging storm themselves.

Jesus' questions are full of meaning for us. The very essence of our being is in His hands. Do we have faith in the One who determines our future? Jesus may not eliminate our fear, but walking intimately with Him will help us to know the Peacemaker and Life Giver at a maturing level of trust, sometimes with a few dips and crests.

Jesus spoke, and the waters were calmed. All sorts of storms come into our lives and put us in the boat with Jesus. Let's not be afraid, but trust the One who can save and deliver us from all that rages around us. May we keep our eyes on the Lord and not on the storm.

Fear Not

NIKI

THE BIBLE TELLS US "DO NOT FEAR" or some variation of those words some three hundred sixty-five times. It's the command God gives in His Word more than any other. Seems God knew we would have a problem with fear.

In the story where this verse is found, Jesus is asleep in a boat with his disciples when a storm hits. Terror grips them as they imagine the boat being shredded by the wind and waves. Fearing for their lives, they urgently awaken Jesus, wondering how He can sleep when their death feels imminent. Terror can grip us the same way when circumstances take a hard turn. Fear can roll in like a hurricane, and we wonder where God is in our distress. Is He sleeping on the job?

Fear tends to show us where our faith is weak.

Have you ever heard of exposure therapy? It's a technique therapists use to help someone overcome their fears. The theory is to expose the person to the very thing they fear, allowing them to see how they're able to safely endure it. Over time, exposure therapy lessens the fear and grows the confidence. If your anxiety is caused by, say, perfectionism, the therapy might be to intentionally fail at something. If you're a kid or teen, you might be instructed to intentionally fail a test. The idea being that you would see the consequences aren't nearly as bad as you had imagined. One test doesn't make you a failure. This kind of therapy allows you to safely see how the outcome of a situation in your mind is likely exaggerated.

Sometimes, I wonder if exposure therapy might be a technique God uses, too. Everything that happens to us passes through God's hands first. If He doesn't cause what happens, He at least allows it. How we react to the circumstances God allows can tell us a lot about our faith. Hard seasons can either make us better by leaning into God and depending on Him for strength or make us bitter by turning away from and blaming God for our difficulties. The choice is ours.

One of the most fearful realizations for me is that nowhere in Scripture does God promise a "storybook ending" to a trying season. He leaves the outcome unknown. It's in this fertile ground of uncertainty that faith grows—trusting in God's goodness when we don't know how things will turn out in the end.

But God does promise strength to stand and endure, and He does promise to meet our needs even in the storms of life. It's on these two promises we can hang our faith in times of trial. God is still on His throne. Though we don't know the outcome of our everyday circumstances, we do know how our story ends—in paradise with our Savior, who never takes His eyes off us as we navigate the sometimes stormy waters of this life.

God, have mercy on me. I am Yours, and You are my only hope.
Thank you, Father, for Your faithfulness to Your promises. Amen.

Day 8

Behold, you delight in truth in the inward being,
and you teach me wisdom in the secret heart.

—*Psalm 51:6*

Is the Light Really Darkness?

NIKI

AS SOON AS I DISCONNECTED the call, I knew. I had spoken an outright lie when my friend questioned me directly about something she suspected I did. What I did was done in ignorance and innocence, but my lie to cover it up made me guilty. It didn't take long for my conscience to convict me.

As many times as I had prayed to hear God's voice, I couldn't ignore it this time. It was the Holy Spirit, loud and clear. I did have quite an argument with Him, though, as He was nudging me to call my friend back, admit to the lie, and ask her forgiveness.

When David wrote Psalm 51, his case was a little different. He'd committed some egregious sins and then tried to cover them up. When that plan failed, it led him to murder. It wasn't his conscience that convicted him, though. It was his friend, Nathan. Once David recognized his sin, he understood he had sinned not only against Bathsheba and Uriah, but ultimately, he had sinned against God. Every sin, even my little lie, is a sin against God.

David learned a lesson about self-deception through the admonition of Nathan. All of us are vulnerable to it. Jesus even warned

32

about it in Luke 11:35, "Therefore be careful lest the light in you be darkness." Rationalizing what we do is a form of self-deception. It may make us feel better in the moment, but it never makes it right. David asked for truth in his heart and wisdom in his conscience. He didn't want to make the same mistake again.

In a later psalm, David prayed God would open his eyes to *any way* that offended the Lord. "Search me, O God, and know my heart! Try me and know my thoughts! And see if there be any grievous way in me, and lead me in the way everlasting" (Psalm 139:23–24). We can pray this same prayer and trust God to answer and forgive.

When I called my friend back, she forgave me. But thinking about it ten years later, I still shudder with the same unease I felt in having to make that call in the first place.

The Movie Moved to a New Theater

CONSTANCE

DOES YOUR HEART HOLD SECRETS you hope no one will ever discover? We don't want to remember that painful moment or the event that brings the humiliation and self-contempt that seems to never go away. We aren't those people anymore; we are redeemed and reclaimed by Christ. That was then, and this is now. We won't tell anyone because we told God, and that's it. But why does it keep coming up in our minds?

Many psychologists embrace the belief that when trauma victims share their stories with another person, or especially in a group, healing occurs more quickly than when carrying the pain in isolation. I have found it to be true. When sharing our trauma, the enemy's power over our lives is broken. The secret we've hidden is revealed, and we're free from the hold it had in our lives.

My dear friend Ellen and I were dining together one evening. Before I knew what was happening, I shared with her a part of my past I had kept hidden for thirty-five years, something that still filled me with regret. I believe God saw the damage it was causing in my life and desired to bring truth and wisdom into the hidden secret places.

When I shared my heart with Ellen that day, I quickly perceived her look of surprise. In that moment, I was filled with shame and humiliation. Would Ellen feel differently about me now? Would she still consider me a friend? Maybe I should have kept my secret sin to myself.

Ellen sensed my anxiety. "Constance, there is nothing you could say or do that would make me not love you. The look on my face was sadness and grief that you had to experience that pain."

I had misjudged her reaction. The openness and vulnerability to understand her reaction instead of letting it fester in my heart and do much more added damage made all the difference. Every emotion possible flowed through my body at her words. My heart and soul were free from the enemy's hold on me that day! I experienced God's unconditional love and understood His desire to set me free. The pain I had carried in my heart alone was now held between Ellen and me; it was being played on a different screen in a new theater.

It takes humility, courage, and the Holy Spirit to move us forward in our stories. He delights in moving us through our stories of redemption and healing. God desires to bring light into the darkness, to bring healing and freedom. Our stories matter to God and to those around us.

Lord, thank You for leading me in wisdom and truth. May I always seek the perfect and good thing from You. Forgive me when I fail. Show me, Lord, the areas of my heart I have yet to surrender. Amen.

Day 9

"And I will give them one heart and a new spirit I will put within them. I will remove the heart of stone from their flesh and give them a heart of flesh."

—Ezekiel 11:19

A Heart Transplant!

CONSTANCE

JUST AS OUR PHYSICAL HEARTS dispense oxygen and vital nutrients throughout our bodies to keep us alive, we also have spiritual hearts that enlighten us with wisdom and guidance for eternal life.

My younger heart of stone was changed in midlife for a heart that seeks after God and His goodness. Before that, I didn't realize how hard and destructive my heart was. But when God invited me into His family and gave me a new heart, I saw the difference. I received a heart transplant! One of the most beautiful things our new hearts do is correct us at times for our benefit.

Recently, I had such an experience. Someone mentioned a particular word that triggered a negative response in me, as I disagreed with the concept this person was presenting. Resistance and anger filled my heart, and I was surprised by the emotional and physical feelings within me. I soon became aware that the Spirit was exposing my heart's attitude. I allowed God to interrupt and inform me with new perspectives, thus allowing my heart and mind to be *reformed* regarding anger. This change of perspective was good and is a benefit of walking closely with God.

The heart is a mixed bag as Luke 6:45 points out. For out of our hearts come love and forgiveness, hope and gratitude, but also hate and every evil thing. Thus, we need a Spirit-led heart to assist in making wise and godly choices. Hopefully, we'll choose movement toward a pure heart seeking God, not a sinful heart full of all sorts of evil.

God cares about our hearts and our spirits. His desire to create a clean heart and a right spirit in us is loving and kind and for our good. Friends, take notice when your heart is full of contentment or when it's being choked with anger or any other mischievous evil. Proverbs 4:23 says, "Keep your heart with all vigilance, for from it flow the springs of life."

Hard as Stone

NIKI

FOR SEVERAL YEARS, I PARTICIPATED in Bible Study Fellowship, a wonderful international program. During one of our small group discussions, the question was asked, "Do you believe God still performs miracles today?" While some struggled to name some modern-day miracles, I needed only to look inside myself. My thoughts went to my own heart. The greatest miracle I've experienced to this day is God changing my heart from hard and stony to tender and responsive, a heart of flesh as Ezekiel calls it.

God is in the heart-changing business. When I think back to my life before my relationship with the Lord, it makes me cringe. While our human nature bends toward sin and selfishness, my hardened heart showed itself in a myriad of other ways, too—like a short temper with coworkers. Relentlessly, I had to make my point of view known, expecting my desires to be met (even at the expense of others' feelings). I never admitted a mistake, deflected blame, and on and on.

During that time, Joe used to joke with friends about how "It's all about Niki." I laughed, too, because it being "all about me" wasn't something I felt needed to change. I rationalized that because I had a traumatic childhood, I didn't have the ability to empathize with anyone. My walls were high and thick and "barbed wiry." Talk about a hard and stony heart!

But God . . . . Aren't those the two greatest words? But God . . . loved me enough to pursue me and capture my heart. He drew me to spend time with Him in His Word, to be still and listen for whatever He wanted to say. Nothing has been the same since. He did put a new Spirit within me, and it has changed everything about me.

And He's not done yet. Sometimes, it's easy to become impatient, because I know I'm not yet fully the person God created me to be. But I'm also no longer the person I used to be. The Holy Spirit working in me—sanctification—is in God's timing and not my own. One day, we all will be exactly who God created us to be.

Have you experienced your own "But God" miracles? All it takes is surrender to Jesus. May we never look back from where we came with regret but look forward with thanksgiving and gratitude for the heart-changing miracles of God.

Abba Father, thank You for your never-ending work in me. Thank You for pursuing me even when my heart was as hard as stone. Thank You for Your deep-seated miracle within me. Help me to live to love You and love others well. Amen.

Day 10

As each has received a gift, use it to serve one another,
as good stewards of God's varied grace.

—*1 Peter 4:10*

Can You Write? Then Write!

NIKI

THE BIBLE TELLS US GOD has given us spiritual gifts, and He also gives us talents. It can often be hard to acknowledge a talent or giftedness in a certain area. It's been that way for me with writing. It can be hard to call oneself a writer. I've heard it said by other writers that if you put words to paper in some form or another you're a writer. Being published doesn't make you a writer; writing makes you a writer. Makes sense.

Endeavoring to write with the goal of bringing your words to the world in published form is another thing altogether. Who am I to think someone wants to hear what I have to say about anything? Self-doubt is a writer's close companion. But those kinds of thoughts don't come from God. Doubt is a weapon Satan loves to wield. He did it first in the garden with Eve when he said, "Did God really say?" He stirred up doubt within her, enough so that she believed him instead of trusting God.

God wants us to be good stewards of our gifts and talents and to use them to serve one another. We're to use our gifts with humility, but we shouldn't be shy about using them. Serving others through our gifts is also serving God, and we're to do it to the best of our ability. "Whatever you do, work heartily, as for the Lord and not for men" (Colossians 3:23).

So, let's resist Satan and his lies of doubt. Truthfully think about the things you do well and embrace your gifts. We can't know how God might use even our smallest effort to shine the light and love of Jesus into this dark world.

What's Your Gift to the World?

CONSTANCE

NIKI AND I ONCE ENROLLED in a six-week class exploring varying genres of art each week—drawing, differing painting styles, pencil art, pottery, etc. We then took a calligraphy class. We were determined to find our artistic gifting and were confident we both had one. Each class was fun (somewhat) but also grueling and often difficult. We concluded we weren't artists, after all. I came away from these classes with an acrylic painting, which I donated to the studio, and the strangest-looking piece of pottery. Niki's masterpiece hung in their garage until it wound up in the waste bin.

Finding one's God-given gift can be just as challenging. I believe we each have something uniquely "us" that God wants to use for the world. I also believe it will be something you're particularly good at and you love doing, a passion that awakens joy in you. There are a number of personality tests, such as Meyers-Briggs and Enneagram, which are helpful for some. I've noticed our circle of friends and family can sometimes see our gifts more easily than we can. Someone once told me, "You are an encourager, Constance." I believe it's true;

I love noticing things about people, even small things, and offering praise and encouragement.

God benevolently bestows gifts to His children. His gift of grace comes to us as we surrender our lives to Him by accepting Jesus' atonement for our sins. Jesus also promised the gift of the Holy Spirit to every believer, a Comforter and Prevailer of truth in our lives. All gifts are to be enjoyed by us and shared with others.

Niki and I finally figured out what we love—writing! We both love journaling, and Niki has previously written a book, *Little Girl Mended,* recounting her story of redemption from childhood abuse. So, God placed it on our hearts to write a book together. We've cherished the experience. It has been both joyful and difficult in so many ways. Writing together has been a gift for each of us and, hopefully, for you, too. Remember every perfect gift comes from the Father (James 1:17). No gift is insignificant in God's eyes.

Benevolent Father and Creator of all things, I receive the gifts You have given me. May I use them for Your work to bless others. Amen.

Day 11

And the Lord spoke to Moses, saying, "Bring the tribe of Levi near, and set them before Aaron the priest, that they may minister to him. They shall keep guard over him and over the whole congregation before the tent of meeting, as they minister at the tabernacle."

—Numbers 3:5–7

And the Lord Spoke

CONSTANCE

DO YOU HAVE A TRIBE OF PEOPLE with whom you "do life" on a regular basis? I'm not speaking of the hundreds of friends on your Facebook page or commenters on your blog or listeners to your podcast. I'm talking about four or five close friends who accept you unconditionally; they see your flaws but also your potential. They celebrate your triumphs and encourage you in your failures. They love you through it all, especially in the muck of life. Support like that matters today, more than ever, if we're going to thrive in these times in which we live.

I believe God knew that we would need support from others. He commissioned Moses to gather the tribe of Levi and place them around Aaron for the purpose of ministering to him and protecting him. This command shows the loving care, attention, and level of commitment God had for Aaron and for those who came before the Tabernacle to be close to the Holy Presence. The tribe of Levi was responsible for Aaron, as our circle of friends care and pray for us and we for them.

When I was going through a painful and stressful season, my church small group loved me unconditionally, fed me, covered me with prayer, and provided for my every need, spiritually and physically. They were my "therapy group" and support. Their encouragement kept me going when I barely knew what I needed . . . but they knew. Daily contact, a walk, dinner or lunch out, and church altars where I poured my heart out to people who prayed continuously for me. Their love and support enabled me to survive. God gave me the support I needed. He can bring a tribe to us, just as He did for Aaron.

Interestingly, in this verse, God spoke to Moses instead of directly to Aaron. Could it be that Aaron was already worn out with responsibility, and God intervened through Moses to assemble the tribe of Levi for him? God is concerned with our well-being and spiritual needs, particularly those of pastors and church leaders who are charged with shepherding their tribes of Christ-followers. Those who faithfully contend for us through times of need and share their guidance and presence need our support as much as Aaron needed the Levites.

"Who's Going to Baptize Him?"

NIKI

IN NUMBERS 3, GOD ESTABLISHED the priesthood with the tribe of Levi. The Levites would serve God in the Tabernacle and assist Aaron who was the first high priest. The priests had a special and significant role to play as intermediaries between a holy God and a sinful people. Only the high priest could enter the Most Holy Place behind the curtain in the Tabernacle and later the Temple. The priests had an intercessory role until Jesus.

A few Christmases ago, my youngest brother and his wife came to stay with us over the holiday. While enjoying dinner on a sunset harbor cruise, my brother surprised me by asking if I would baptize him. What a privilege to be a part of my brother's journey! It gave me such hope to see him turn away from a more works-based belief and want to know Jesus in a deeper way.

We planned his baptism for the upcoming summer, when our extended family would all be together at a lake house in the North Carolina mountains. This cold lake would be our baptismal. The morning my brother had chosen found him battling his nerves. The rest of our family was still entrenched in works-based, manmade-rules religion. He asked me to tell the family what we were about to do. So, I did. Most everyone looked at me with shock. One of my nephews-in-law spoke up and said, "Who's going to baptize him? There isn't a priest here." Ah, what a perfect opportunity to explain how the death and resurrection of Jesus made us all priests, that we no longer need an ordained priest to be the intercessor between us and God. "But you are a chosen race, a royal priesthood . . . ." (1 Peter 2:9).

With Christ's last breath, the curtain in the Temple, separating the Most Holy Place where only the high priest could enter, was torn in two, from top to bottom, signifying we are no longer separated from God and can come before Him on our own with no need of a priest as intermediary. "So let us come boldly to the throne of our gracious God. There we will receive his mercy, and we will find grace to help us when we need it most" (Hebrews 4:16 NLT).

My family watched from the shore as my brother, his wife, and I walked down the slick bank into the water. Before we baptized him, he confessed his belief in Jesus. He went under the water and was raised to new life in Christ. No one in our family asked us more about the baptism or what I had told them about it, priests, and us. But . . . a seed could have been planted that God will later harvest.

Dear God, may I know when to be friend to someone in need. Help me to gather together a community of believers who will love me throughout my life and I them. Thank You for making a way to come directly to Your throne. Amen.

Day 12

I rejoice at your word like one who finds great spoil.
—Psalm 119:162

Gathering Dust

NIKI

GROWING UP, I DISTINCTLY REMEMBER the large family Bible we had. It had a brown leather cover embossed with Holy Bible in gold and probably weighed ten pounds. It was impressive! But in all my nineteen years living at home, I never once saw any of the eight of us crack open the cover to read even one word. It sat on the bottom shelf of an end table in the living room, and the only time it was touched was when someone noticed it covered with a thick layer of dust. How sad we had the very voice of God in our midst, and we ignored Him. We believed in God, but we relied on Sunday church services to tell us what He said.

Everything changed a couple of years after I moved out and was married. My new brother-in-law began talking to me about the Bible, and I soon discovered God actually intends for us to read it, to spend time in it, to meditate on what He says to us through it. It was difficult to understand at first, but the more time I spent with the Lord in Scripture, the more He revealed.

Spending time with the Father in the truth of His Word is one of the important elements to becoming more Christ-like. Do you believe the Word is alive and relevant today? From Genesis to Revelation, it reveals Jesus and explains God's plan for man's redemption. But for those who don't know Jesus, the Bible seems like foolishness. Paul wrote a powerful statement in his letter to the church in Corinth: "For the word of the cross is folly to those who are perishing, but to us who are being saved it is the power of God" (1 Corinthians 1:18).

There is power in the pages of your Bible. David, an Israelite king who wrote almost half of the book of Psalms, rejoiced over God's Word because he knew it was a treasure greater than any earthly one. We who are saved know God's Word is truth, cover to cover. Jesus promised we can and will know the truth.

Friends, try to cultivate the habit of spending some daily time with the Lord in His Word. It will change your world as you tap into God's power in His pages. Read it, journal, meditate on it. I promise, nothing in this world comes close to the treasure of experiencing the presence of God through time with Him in His Word. David knew it and so can we.

My Help Comes From the Lord

CONSTANCE

THIS MORNING WHEN READING THIS Scripture, I asked my husband, Carroll, what it meant to him. He replied, "You've got me as your spoil," without even a blink of the eye! We chuckled as I looked at him and smiled. You see, I was a single mom for five years before I met Carroll. The battles won during those years led to an unexpected marriage full of blessings for Sebastian and me. Carroll truly is my spoil!

What does rejoicing mean to us who read the Word daily in our devotional practice? The psalmist encourages us to ponder the many benefits he has experienced in his own life. I'm reminded of God's mercy when I have failed miserably and how He has steadied my steps when I was prone to wander down pathways I shouldn't. When my tears flooded my pillow at night in anguish, He was there. When reminded of my failures, the Word spoke, "You are my beloved," to me. At times when I didn't have the resources I needed as a single parent, God spoke to others to provide. How happy I was when Carroll came into my life, and I was no longer doing it alone. Our lives became one shared life experience. I was thankful to have a companion and a father for my son. God has been generous to us.

My life is full of many years, and I pray for more opportunities for God to display His mercy, grace, and love. I have a lifetime of experiences and a chest full of redemption. I imagine you do too. We enjoy great bounty (spoil) from His generosity and benevolence, calm in the midst of chaos, healing, and much more.

When we find ourselves in the mire of life, the Word refreshes us like nothing else. We leap as sheep with hope and excitement that our Father has heard our cry and is intimately answering through His Holy Spirit.

In catastrophic times, we're comforted and rejoice in His presence. When our kids are going through testing, we can trust in the promise of God's Word: " . . . the offspring of the righteous will be delivered" (Proverbs 11:21b). In times of blessing, and there are many, we rejoice in God's goodness toward us.

God's Word is a lamp to our feet, a breath of freshness to our souls, a comfort when needed, a deliverance from our distress, and more. Recall His Word written for those long ago but applicable to us today through the Holy Spirit. The Word is living, powerful, and present.

Father God, thank You for the gift of Your Scriptures.
Help me to organize my day to allow time with
You. Speak to me clearly through Your Word, Lord,
and give me wisdom to understand. Amen.

Day 13

*Even in laughter the heart may ache, and
the end of joy may be grief.*
—Proverbs 14:13

A Broken Wrist Can Be a Time of Joy

CONSTANCE

WHILE AT MY FIRST AEROBICS exercise class at a senior center, music filled the speakers, and we began stepping up and down to the beat. About five minutes in, I miscalculated the step onto the platform and fell, landing on my wrist. I knew my bone was broken. In excruciating pain, I could see my hand and arm were no longer aligned. At the hospital, an X-ray confirmed what I already knew. Holding my arm close to my body, I anticipated how my life was going to be much different in the coming weeks without the use of my right hand.

Interestingly, the weeks that followed were not as I anticipated. In my entire career, I had never had so much time off work. I learned to do things differently, including writing with my left hand. My recovery allowed for longer walks during the day, more time in prayer, physical therapy, and afternoon naps. The broken wrist turned into one of the best breaks of my life.

Sometimes things happen that turn our joyful hearts to heartache. Other times, our heartache turns to laughter sooner than we imagine. Someone once said, "How we handle the hard times is how we handle life." If each challenging experience pulls us into worry, then we'll likely live a life of worry. But if we manage the things of this fallen world with reliance on the Holy Spirit, our Comforter, we have a better chance of living with hope and joy.

Life can be tough. We all have our challenges but also stories of joy and redemption. The Creator is still creating. He knows your name, and He knows your story. He loves you deeply.

Humorous Disguises

NIKI

AFTER FORTY-EIGHT YEARS TOGETHER, there isn't much conflict in our marriage these days. But many years ago, there was a conflict. Hurtful words were spoken, and my heart was heavy. Soon after hearing those words, I went out to dinner with friends. My heart ached, but I laughed along with everyone else that night. No one suspected a thing. In the back seat of the car on the ride home, while holding back tears, I lamented to myself how I wished I could be as carefree and happy as my friends. But you know what? I don't know what their laughter may have been covering up for them.

I grew up in a household that kept family issues inside our four walls—good, bad, or ugly. It can be a hard habit to break. Ask me how I am, and I'll say, "Fine!" or even "Great!" Sometimes it's true, and other times, not so much. Put on a good face. It's what a lot of us do when we walk out the door and into the world. It can be so much easier to paste on a smile and laugh in all the right places than to open up wounds by sharing them with someone else. Humor can be a potent self-defense mechanism.

We never know what pain someone may be walking through or

whether they are hiding behind a wall of laughter. A kind word may be just what they need to keep going. Words matter. The happy-go-lucky cashier or the grumpy person behind you in line may be carrying a heavy load of pain. You've probably heard the saying, "Hurt people, hurt people." While that saying may carry some truth, hurt people also hide behind smiles and laughter. For our part as followers of Jesus, we're to love people, whether they hide behind laughter or allow us into their hurt. May we allow the Holy Spirit to have His way in us. His fruit—love, joy, peace, patience, kindness, goodness, faithfulness, gentleness, and self-control—will give us all we need to love people the way Jesus does.

My marriage did make it through that conflict so long ago and a few others since. Just as love covers a multitude of sins, forgiveness covers a multitude of hurts, even those disguised with laughter.

Most Holy Father, in the grief and heartache I carry,
let me experience abundant joy and laughter to lighten
my spirit. Remind me You are with me, and that You
hold it all together. Tomorrow is a new day. Amen.

Day 14

And the Lord said to Joshua, "Do not be afraid of them, for tomorrow at this time I will give over all of them, slain, to Israel."

—*Joshua 11:6a*

Satan's Weapon

NIKI

WHEN I WAS THIRTEEN, the tenants renting our upstairs apartment moved out, and I moved my bedroom up to that floor. I was thrilled to have the space of the apartment but also a bit afraid of being by myself and removed from the rest of the family. One hot summer night, as I lay in bed, hoping for a breeze to come through the open windows, I heard a noise sounding like it came from right outside my door. My door was at the top of a staircase leading up from the outside back door. I heard the noise again. With a fear like I'd never before known, I crept to the door. I quietly turned the lock. Silently counting one . . . two . . . three, I pulled the door open in a flash, hoping to surprise whoever was on the other side. Nothing but utter blackness! I couldn't see anything for the complete darkness in the stairway. With pounding heart, I slammed and locked the door. As I quickly made my way back to my bed, I passed by the open bathroom window and heard the sound again. Only then did I realize it was coming from outside on the street and not outside my door. I almost laughed, but fear had a tight grip on me that night.

Joshua knew the feeling of gut-wrenching fear, too. God chose him to replace Moses and lead His people into the Promised Land. He had to be a warrior to accomplish God's purpose. He defeated thirty-one kings and waged war for a long time, yet what I notice is how many times God tells Joshua not to be afraid but to be courageous. God knew a little something about Joshua's character. He knew he would need to be reminded not to fear, and He knows the same about us. God knows us, and He also knows Satan.

Fear is one of the greatest weapons Satan uses against us. It far too often keeps us from accomplishing our purpose. Have you heard the saying "paralyzed with fear"? It's a weapon in Satan's hands. If Satan can't get us to turn against God, the next best thing is to paralyze us with fear, rendering us ineffective in God's plan to witness to the world. If Satan can't have us, he'll settle for having the ones we might have reached for Jesus had we not been afraid.

How can we overcome fear? "There is no fear in love, but perfect love casts out fear" (1 John 4:18). The antidote to fear is love, and God is love. The deeper we know and trust God, the less we'll struggle with fear. Draw near to Him. He loves you, cares for you, and is with you always. Let the Lord fill you with His perfect love and then walk out into the world courageous!

Oh, How I Need You!

CONSTANCE

WHEN SEBASTIAN WAS THREE YEARS old, he had bacterial meningitis. For three days, he was in a coma, and then for three more days, one side of his body was paralyzed. Powerless to fix his condition, I was desperately afraid.

One afternoon, a woman I had never met before approached me

in the ICU. She reached out and held my arms, saying, "You must not be afraid. Ask God to give you peace, and He will." The words she spoke seemed strange at first, but they gave me hope to believe it was possible to have peace and not be afraid. I was desperate for hope. I went to the restroom and cried out to God for peace and to heal my son. Suddenly, I felt the warmth of God's presence pour over me like liquid from the top of my head and down my body. From that moment on, even though Sebastian was still in a coma, I had peace that all would be well. I didn't feel the same anxiety I had. I looked for the woman who had spoken to me just minutes before. I asked the nurses if they saw her, but was told no one had been in the area at all. Forty-four years ago, I believed I had an encounter with an angel of the Lord, and I still believe it today.

Numerous times in the Bible, God tells his people not to be afraid—even his fiercest warriors, like Joshua. His words are full of hope, encouragement, and strength. "Have I not commanded you? Be strong and courageous. Do not be frightened, and do not be dismayed, for the Lord your God is with you wherever you go" (Joshua 1:9). What we have to decide is whether we have the *courage to trust* God to do what He says He'll do.

I have faith and strength until something challenging hits my life. Then suddenly, I find myself lying in a puddle of tears and hopelessness. I'm working on that struggle. But what I hold onto most is that when I have needed Him most, I have heard the sweet sound of my Lord whisper in my heart, saying, *Do not be afraid, Constance. I am still here with you.* I have learned that when I am powerless, my only option is to trust God. Sebastian survived; his body was healed, for which I'm profoundly grateful; and I experienced the goodness of the Lord.

What do you need to trust God for today?

Father, draw me near, open my heart, and pour Yourself in. Help me to know You more deeply, in ways that will crush fear and allow me to live fully in Your perfect love. Amen.

Day 15

Indeed, all who desire to live a godly life in
Christ Jesus will be persecuted.

—*2 Timothy 3:12*

Wow! That Really Hurt!

CONSTANCE

JESUS TOLD US THAT THE GREATEST commandments are to love God and to love our neighbors as ourselves. We aren't perfect, but that is our mission. So what's the issue here? Why the backlash on Christianity? We see it, and we experience it ourselves, even within our own families at times and in the world at large.

There seemed to be a trend; early Christians were martyred for their faith. Some met their death in Roman arenas made for entertainment, while others were crucified on crosses as Jesus was. Stephen was the first martyred Christian, and many of the disciples died for the sake of the gospel. We may not be called to martyrdom, but we are called to Christ who lives in us, for our lives are buried in Him and raised to live with Him in eternity.

Many of us have endured brutal trials, distress from family members/friends, or abusive work environments. Others are victims of hate because of their faith. Current school and college environments can be extremely toxic for Christian students because of their religious beliefs. Persecution is never easy; it is, however, our testimony of deep commitment to Christ because He has radically changed our lives.

Paul, familiar with persecution, understood the cost of the crucifixion of Jesus, as well as the blessing of the resurrection, the gift of eternal life. This is the good news of the gospel of salvation. There are many reasons we suffer for our faith—our passion for Jesus, the confidence we enjoy that He is the only way to the Father, the way God helps us to live a life of putting Him first and loving our neighbors as ourselves. I'm reminded that Jesus experienced the fullness of humanity from birth to adulthood to death. He lived and died so we can partake, as He did, in a resurrected life. We will die, but we will rise! The grief of death becomes the greatest joy of life everlasting. Jesus is evidence of this reality.

Only the Holy Spirit can draw others to Jesus. He pursued and drew me. I'm thankful for His mercy and grace, for a resurrection life on earth.

The Power of Pain

NIKI

WEDNESDAY, AUGUST 12, 2020, at 3:30 in the afternoon, my family's life changed with a single telephone call. We couldn't know at the time, but that phone call began a years-long season of suffering the likes of which none of us had ever before experienced. One of my beloved family members became the target of a false accusation. We spent a year and a half waiting for justice from the judicial system, which by the grace of God finally came. Then we spent another year and a half dealing with the unremitting evil of the accuser. Satan had my family in his sights.

Jesus told us to expect trouble in this life, and in 2 Timothy 3:12, Paul reiterates that walking closely with and in obedience to the Lord draws the attention of Satan. Satan has no need to interfere in the life of someone who lives far from the Lord with nary a thought about Him. Since Satan knows he can't hurt God Himself, he satisfies his evil longings with trying to hurt those closest to the Lord.

Since He is sovereign over all things, nothing happens to us without God's permission. That's a hard truth to hear about a God who is always good and loves us unfailingly. But our loving God never expects us to stand up to Satan's onslaught alone. The power in a painfully dark, evil season is the nearness of God in the darkness. Have you ever experienced how you can hear God more easily and more clearly during the painful, trying times of life? It's not an illusion. It's because God, if we let Him, can be closest in the trials.

Pain is a great magnifier. It not only magnifies God's nearness but also His character. It's been my experience that God reveals parts of Himself through our suffering that we could not and would not know otherwise. Coming to know God in ways you've yet to experience Him is worth any length of suffering or pain. Truly.

There's another powerful insight to a painful experience I'm just beginning to understand. Before our trauma began in 2020, life was good, comfortable. I can look back through the lens of hindsight, though, and see it to be somehow shallow, superficial. Now, through this experience of raw pain, life has deeper meaning. We've walked closely with God through a terribly dark experience. We know what it feels like to be carried in His strong arms and know only He is keeping us upright.

Would I wish for a season like these last few years? Never. But I can honestly say I'm thankful to have been drawn closer to the Lord than I've ever been, to have learned to be in constant communion with Him, to keep bringing my mind and heart back to Jesus. All are powerful blessings in suffering.

Holy God, thank You for the blessings You bring through suffering.
Thank You for Your never failing presence and Your strength. Amen.

Day 16

"I know your works, your toil and your patient endurance, and how you cannot bear with those who are evil, but have tested those who call themselves apostles and are not, and found them to be false."

—*Revelation 2:2*

I Know Something You Don't Know

NIKI

MY TWO SONS ARE GROWN MEN now, but when they were little tykes, they sometimes bickered as siblings do. My boys are only twenty months apart in age. They loved each other fiercely, and they sometimes hated each other just as much. Often in those moments of battle, my role morphed into referee more than mom. Inevitably, I would try to figure out who the guilty one was who started the fray. Each one blamed the other, and on it went. There was no way for me to know who did what, much less why.

Being in that kind of dark, so to speak, is a problem Jesus never has. Have you ever noticed how each of the letters to the seven churches in Revelation begins with the words "I know"? Take a look at Revelation 2 and 3, and you'll see it—all seven letters. Jesus knows! He never has to wonder who did what and why. It's true of the seven churches, and it's true of us.

Why then do we try to hide anything from the Lord? After Adam and Eve sinned, the first thing they did was try to hide themselves from God. We often have the same reaction to our sin. We want to hide our sin from everyone, including God. Because Jesus already bore the punishment for our sins, God always offers forgiveness, but He tells us to confess our sins, not only to Him, but also to one another. Why, though, if He already knows? Because confession is for our sake, not for God's. It's a reminder to us of just how much we need a Savior. Confession also breaks our pride. It's impossible to confess a failure (sin) and hold onto pride at the same time. Confession requires humility, which is a character trait God values.

There's no good purpose in trying to hide from the Lord. He already knows. He knows our hearts better than we do ourselves. May we always come to Him humbly in our confession, confident in His forgiveness, mercy, and grace. Just as Jesus knows us fully, we can fully trust His unfailing love for us. "There is therefore now no condemnation for those who are in Christ Jesus" (Romans 8:1). Yes and amen!

Patient Endurance

CONSTANCE

JESUS SPOKE TO JOHN IN REVELATION through a vision when giving a sharp critique of the church in Ephesus, yet commending them for their patient endurance and steadfastness. The interesting point is Jesus saw everything in their lives. He saw the good deeds, the things they struggled with, the difficulties they walked through, the victories they won. The same is true for us. Jesus sees our work for the Kingdom. He delights when we overcome the enemy's attacks, but He also sees our wounded spirits and broken souls. Nothing is hidden from Him—not our heartbreaks and challenges, broken dreams, wayward children, failed marriages and businesses, nor when our love for Him and our neighbor isn't what it used to be. He sees, He cares, and He prays for us.

John was familiar with the hardships and imprisonments that came because of his beliefs and understood, as Jesus did, the cost for those who believed and stood against the evil in the world. He was full of zeal but also compassionate and humble.

John wrote five books in the New Testament—letters of encouragement and godly instruction to the early churches, as well as warning of evil forces at work in the world to hinder the work Jesus began. John warned them to be aware, as many were infiltrating the early church with false teachings and deceptions.

As a young Christian, I trusted what others told me to believe. As my discernment grew, because of the work of the Holy Spirit, I developed a sensitivity to certain things. My gut was letting me know something was not quite right. I had questions and curiosity and would ask God for wisdom. God wants us to seek the truth, ponder those things we don't totally understand, and take our questions to Him. He will give us clarity in the moment or in the future.

No matter what we face in this earthly life, let's not lose our first love, the love of God who is always present. May we stand strong in our armor as Jesus stood against Satan's attacks. We may have some battle scars, but with God's strength, we can remain faithful to the end.

My Father, I'm grateful that You reveal the things I need to correct. Thank You for the forgiveness of my every sin. I'm grateful You are my constant loving companion throughout my life, leading and guiding me in the way I should walk. Amen.

Day 17

"And there was a widow in that city who kept coming to him and saying, 'Give me justice against my adversary.' For a while he refused . . . 'yet because this widow keeps bothering me, I will give her justice . . . .'" And the Lord said, "Hear what the unrighteous judge says. And will not God give justice to his elect who cry to him day and night? Will he delay long over them? I tell you, he will give justice to them speedily. Nevertheless, when the Son of Man comes, will he find faith on earth?"

—*Luke 18:3–8*

Our Groans for Justice Will Be Answered

CONSTANCE

IN FEBRUARY 2023, A CATASTROPHIC earthquake occurred in Turkey and Syria, killing thousands of people. The agony of the situation left many questioning how to pray about something so devastating and hopeless. Just as the woman who came repeatedly before the unrighteous judge, we can petition God for justice and relief from ongoing trials in this world.

Paul writes in Romans 8 about a world needing to be set free from its bondage to corruption and death. "The Spirit himself intercedes for us with groanings too deep for words" (Romans 8:26). In times when our wordless prayers are laments of the heart for a world full of pain, rest assured, God hears. Like the woman in Luke 18, be diligent and persistent in prayer—God hears our cries. In the wait time, though, God may choose a different answer than what we asked for. Will we be prepared to accept His will when the answer is different from the request?

The need for a righteous Judge, a Savior, is great in our world. We may find ourselves saying, "What's the use? Nothing will change." Have faith, persist, trust God, and keep asking. Prayer is powerful. We aren't alone! Creation is fully anticipating a new earth, one without sin and death. We're longing for redemption and a safer, more beautiful life free from sickness, disease, and death. God promised justice will be given. Even the unrighteous judge finally gave the widow justice over her adversary. Can't we then expect a righteous Judge to deliver justice to His children? Justice will come, either in this life or in eternity. Let's be faithful in the waiting and learn to trust in God's perfect timing.

Jesus asks if He will find faith on earth when He returns? Let's show Him we are a people of faith and prayer. May our groans be, "Lord Jesus, have mercy on us all." He is coming. Be ready and not afraid. Hold on to your faith, for redemption draws near!

Heavenly Father . . .

NIKI

YOU'VE PROBABLY HEARD THE SAYING, "The squeaky wheel gets the grease." In other words, to stop the noise, take care of what the wheel needs. This sentiment seems to be what Jesus is saying in this parable of the widow who kept coming to the judge. Eventually, to get some peace, the judge addresses her concerns. But does God really work that way? Does He answer only those who shout the loudest

65

and the longest? Friends, I don't believe that's what Jesus is saying at all. The parable shows the *contrast* between the judge and the Lord.

Jesus encourages us to pray persistently, but to also know that as soon as we bring Him a request that aligns with His will, He is working. Then why is there often a delay in receiving an answer to our prayers? A delay doesn't mean God isn't working; it means preparation is happening. God answers our requests only when the timing is best, both for His purpose and for us. Faith during the wait is a growing, maturing faith.

I've been bringing a specific prayer to God for years, and I'm still waiting on an answer. Sometimes, I want to give up on this prayer, because I know God has heard it many times. At times, I've asked, "God, you know my heart. You know what this prayer means to me, and I know it aligns with Your will. Should I keep bringing it to You?" It remains heavy on my heart, so I keep praying. He wants us to lay all of our cares on Him, and this care is one I find heaviest to carry. So, I bring it to Him again and again. As I wait for God to move, I continue to remind myself that He's working in ways I can't yet see. Reminding myself to pray repeatedly is for me, not for the Lord. He never needs reminding. He hears and knows even before I bring the prayer to Him.

God instructs us to pray without ceasing. Always having a prayer in our hearts comes from having a heart aligned with His. We're able to commune with God without using words—heart to heart. This kind of unceasing prayer comes only through a committed relationship with the Lord. He's pursuing that kind of relationship with you right this moment. Spend time with Him. Open your heart, and invite Him in.

Almighty and Powerful God, help me to always trust that You hear me and are working on my requests and in my heart. I pray for faith that is strong and determined, not weak and fleeting. I love You, Lord. Amen.

Day 18

*Now to him who is able to do far more abundantly than all that
we ask or think, according to the power at work within us . . . .*
—*Ephesians 3:20*

Dynamic Dynamite!

NIKI

THE FIRST PART OF THIS VERSE seems to be the focus for many of us. How God provides more than we could ask or imagine; how He surprises us with going beyond what we hoped or asked in prayer. We're reminded of God's generosity toward us, His grace, His mercy. But, it's the second half that strikes me—"according to the power at work within us." Because we have the power of the Holy Spirit within us, God is able to *use us* far more than we would ever think we could be used and all to the glory of Jesus!

Have you ever witnessed anyone who is able to speak just the right words to someone in their moment of need? Maybe that person with the right words was you, and you wondered where those words came from. I've had that experience myself. I was able to love and encourage someone with what they needed to hear in that moment. Afterward, I knew what transpired was the work of the Holy Spirit because I had no idea what needed to be said. On another occasion, I witnessed a mission trip teammate do the same with an obscure passage of Scripture that bound up the emotional wounds of someone in pain. Afterward, I told her how amazed I was and asked how she was able to recall a little-known Scripture that perfectly addressed such a deep need. "That wasn't me," she said. "That was the Holy Spirit. I didn't even know I knew that Scripture!" Small examples, but holy power, nonetheless.

That power is the same power Paul writes of here—the Holy Spirit. The word "power" in this verse is the Greek word *dunamis,* from which we get our words *dynamic* and *dynamite.* "Dynamic dynamite" gives a vivid word picture of the power of the Holy Spirit, the power within us. Let's not go through life being unaware of the Holy Spirit's indwelling. Sadly, it's possible. Jesus promised us a Helper and an Advocate, and He delivered on that promise in the Holy Spirit. Yet, it's so easy to live life unattuned to the Spirit's guidance and help. You have the power of dynamic dynamite within you. Draw near to God by consistently spending time with Him in His Word, in prayer, and in worship. He will open your heart to humbly follow where the Spirit leads, and you'll be amazed!

More Than You Can Imagine

CONSTANCE

CARROLL ARRIVED HOME ONE AFTERNOON to share his great news with me. "You've always wanted me to plan a trip, so I have. We're going on a cruise!" I *have* always wanted him to come up with an adventure; however, a cruise was never on my bucket list. My heart seized as anxiety climbed upward in my chest. Wanting to applaud his intentions, I reluctantly said, "Oh, that's wonderful, honey."

Two weeks prior to our adventure, my joy meter hadn't moved. Aware of my lack of excitement, Niki prayed that this trip would be amazing, that I'd be proud of Carroll for planning it, and that the cruise would be more wonderful than I imagined.

My adventure began with jet lag, fatigue, ship disorientation, and dining with strangers with whom I wasn't interested in speaking (I'm embarrassed to admit). I was probably acting like a spoiled child. But it gets better. Our neighbors were arguing loudly for hours in the middle of the night. I gave them grace the first night, but the second night, I went out into the hallway to check their room number. My door slammed shut, and I was locked out in my nightie. At last, the steward came along but wouldn't open my door as I had no identification. After pounding on my door to no avail, the steward telephoned our room. Carroll finally awoke and opened the door looking like a deer in headlights. What in the world was I doing outside our room?

On about day three, trying desperately to find the positive and anticipate the best, things began to change, just like when a large ship turns about in a small area. The prayers kicked in, and the real adventure began! Strangers became friends, the comedian was actually funny, the spa treatment eased the tension in my body, the folks next door stopped screaming, I was sleeping well, and the Aegean blue-green water outside my glass doors captured my heart. When we docked in the gorgeous small town of Kusadasi, Turkey, where Ephesus ruins can be found, a joyful spirit of gratitude and praise filled my heart to overflowing. It was a new day to explore.

God abundantly gave me more than I ever imagined. Even the challenges became funny stories. Sometimes, life is hard for a time, and rest can't be found. Then, my reluctant trip happened at just the right time because God knew what I needed. The Holy Spirit within brought it all together beautifully!

Father, Son, and Holy Spirit, have Your way with me and in me. Help me to be attuned to Your guidance, direction, and power within me. Use me, Lord, like only You can do! Amen.

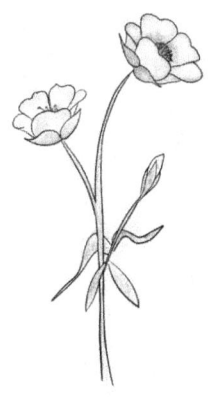

Day 19

Jesus said to her, "Woman, why are you weeping? Whom are you seeking?" Supposing him to be the gardener, she said to him, "Sir, if you have carried him away, tell me where you have laid him, and I will take him away." Jesus said to her, "Mary." She turned and said to him in Aramaic, "Rabboni!" (which means Teacher).

—John 20:15–16

The Moment You Know

CONSTANCE

A FRIEND OF MINE LOST HER son to a drug overdose while she and her husband were away on vacation. Three months later, she was diagnosed with breast cancer, underwent a mastectomy, and received various cancer treatments. Her grief was raw, the death of her son far worse than the cancer in her body.

The ensuing grief after the death of a loved one shakes a person to the core. It disrupts our souls, brings confusion and disbelief, and messes with our concentration. Our ability to make sense of what is happening is impaired for months, sometimes years.

The Gospels give glimpses of the heartbreaking loss after Jesus' death for those closely acquainted with Him. Jesus often spoke of His mission, death, and resurrection. But when it happened, those close to Him seemed surprised and deeply troubled. His death changed everything. They must have pondered, *How are we going to move the ministry forward now that Jesus is gone?*

Not immediately recognizing Jesus in their midst—Mary Magdalene at the tomb, the disciples fishing, and the men on the road to Emmaus—all experienced Jesus as he was before and encountered Him again through His words and actions (John 20 and 21, Luke 24). His resurrection gave them a way forward.

The resurrection happened! Maybe your sadness and grief is hindering your vision. Open your eyes and see the resurrected Jesus who is not only by your side but also in your heart. Jesus will get your attention for sure. Anticipate it, believe it, and receive it today. He's reminding you of His everlasting love and presence always. He is calling your name.

What's in a Name?

NIKI

THE COVER OF THIS BOOK says Niki Krauss, but believe it or not, my given name is Monica. However, my father called me Niki when I was just a year old. It stuck, and so I've been Niki my entire life. If someone calls me Monica, it takes me a second to realize they mean me, and it gives me an unsettled feeling to be called by a name I don't recognize. Names are important. They come to represent who we are, not only to others but also to ourselves.

In these verses, Mary is distressed at finding Christ's tomb empty. She's weeping and distraught when she turns and sees Jesus. She doesn't recognize Him until He calls her name, "Mary." Can you sense the relief that floods her heart and body when Jesus calls her by name? Can you sense the love and compassion in Christ's voice? In the calling of *her* name, she's suddenly able to identify *Him*. How just like God to do the unexpected!

There are many verses in Scripture where God says He calls *us* by name and *knows* us by name. The Lord even calls the stars by name. One of my favorite verses about names is Isaiah 49:16. The New Living Translation reads, "See, I have written your name on the palms of my hands . . . ." I hear the same love and compassion in this verse that Mary heard when Jesus said her name. I imagine our names engraved on Jesus with the nails that went through Him into that rough-hewn wood. It was for us that He shed His blood. There is no greater love.

Truth be told, I've sometimes wondered what God will call me in heaven since I have two names, and the one that feels like me is not my given name. I'm counting on the promise Jesus made in Revelation 2:17, ". . . and I will give him a white stone, with a new name written on the stone that no one knows except the one who receives it." We're already identified as belonging to God because of Jesus. We bear Christ's name in being called Christian. Do you wonder what name will be written on your own white stone?

Father, I pray I always notice You in my day, in both the little and big things of life. I so often call on Your name! Thank You for hearing me every time I do. Amen.

Day 20

"For the thing that I fear comes upon me,
and what I dread befalls me."
—*Job 3:25*

Pain Is A-Comin'

NIKI

JOE WAS A 24-YEAR CAREER U.S. Marine. In the early years of his career and our marriage, he deployed often to Japan for six months at a time. The Marine Corps didn't send families to accompany the Marine on these kind of "short" deployments. So, I found myself at home with a toddler and an infant as a single parent for months at a time.

The pain of his departure was deep. After my first experience with that pain, and knowing it would come again and again, I found myself fearing and dreading the next deployment. The fear and dread manifested itself in me in withdrawal. My subconscious mind deduced that if I withdrew emotionally for the month before Joe deployed, the pain of his leaving would somehow be less when the time came. It never worked out that way. I eventually came to recognize what I was doing, but I still couldn't stop myself from trying to protect my heart in this way.

My experience makes this verse in Job very interesting to me. Even though (or maybe even because) Job's life was so blessed, he carried a fear in the back of his mind of calamity coming. Expecting the "other shoe to drop" gives us the illusion we'll be prepared if calamity does hit. But living with that kind of anxiety takes away from the joy of living in this moment, in the present.

In the fear and the dread is also a quest to hang on to some feeling of control. In mentally preparing for some future trial, we're already relying on our own strength to get us through what hasn't even happened yet. Where is our trust and reliance on God's strength in that? If we trust in God's promise to strengthen and carry us always, we don't need to mentally and emotionally prepare for some future event that may never come to pass.

I never did fully learn that lesson in our early Marine Corps years. Now, decades later, by His grace, I know God more deeply and know I can trust Him with my future instead of carrying it myself and stealing away the joy of living in the present. And I know you can trust Him, too.

Faith Smashes Fear

CONSTANCE

JOB, A RIGHTEOUS MAN DEVOTED to God, had concern for his children's behavior. He regularly consecrated them to God just in case they had sinned. Worry can evolve into fear. Job's life was about to crumble. He would lose his health, beloved children, prosperity, everything. Was he living a fearful life while living in prosperity? I imagine many of us experience a life of blessings while struggling with fear and peace as Job did.

Who hasn't been caught in a cycle of fear? Fear of the unknown, serious illness, death, loneliness, and on and on. I used to cringe when the phone rang and displayed a particular number. My heart

76

would beat rapidly as I feared bad news on the other end. It usually was. Fear had its claws on my mind, and panic gripped my heart. I couldn't shake the deathly grip fear had on my soul. Oh, how I could relate to Job's fear!

The path of fear is destructive and paralyzes us from living the abundant life God has for us. A life based on faith and trust grows hope. Hope breathes life into our expectant prayers and produces outcomes that are more than we can imagine! I decided that was the kind of life I would live. My fear response never fixed anything—not the person calling or me. When the phone rang again, I flipped the script, so to speak. I veered off the seasoned path of fear onto the firmer road of trust, to trust the One who cares more deeply than even I for the person on the other end of the telephone line. I chose to put my complete trust in Jesus and live from faith not in fear. Surrendering to Jesus is a daily practice for me, a reminder of who is in control. Faith smashes fear!

Do we indulge fear instead of faith when something rocks our lives to the core and everything is threatened? Our minds are the steering wheels that drive the "what if" scenarios of doom. Let's choose to steer our hearts toward faith. Today, may our prayers be faith-filled and promise-driven in the One who creates new beginnings.

Lord, help me to always live in the present moment—fully relying on You, right here, right now—and to leave the future moments in Your hands where they belong. Amen.

Day 21

"The wind blows where it wishes, and you hear its sound,
but you do not know where it comes from or where it goes.
So it is with everyone who is born of the Spirit."

—*John 3:8*

Swinging Leaves and Spirit Wonderings

CONSTANCE

ONE SUMMER MORNING, I WAS mesmerized by the trees outside my window, some leaves swinging wildly in the wind while others hung motionless. Why did the wind affect a certain branch and not others? But the same is true with tornados and hurricanes, often destroying one side of the street and yet not a single home on the other side.

Evidence of the wind is seen in the swaying of the leaves, just as evidence of the Spirit in a person is seen in a life changed—the way we live, our love for God and our neighbors, the inspiration of the Word speaking to us. We hear His promptings in our spirit. Ask yourself, *Am I the same person I was five years ago, one year ago, one month ago?* If we allow Him, the Spirit of God will move us to the place we need to be, and we may not even know it's happening until we look back and see from where we came.

Jesus uses the wind as an analogy to spark Nicodemus to think outside his traditional Jewish upbringing, which included extensive study of God's Word. He was a Pharisee and later a member of the

Jewish Council in Jerusalem. Nicodemus knew of Jesus' miracles, things he knew only God could do. Was Jesus the Messiah? It confused Nicodemus when Jesus said he must be born again, not from flesh but from the Spirit. When someone accepts Jesus and is filled with the Holy Spirit, they know in their heart something is different. Yet, it's impossible to truly measure and explain how everything has changed. Just as the wind blows where it wishes by the power of its Creator, the work of the Holy Spirit in a person is supernatural.

Those swinging, bug-eaten leaves hanging from limbs, somehow sensing autumn approaching, fall to the ground, decay, and nourish the tree roots. Then spring returns with new shades of green, and life moves forward. There is so much beauty in the mystery of life. Be open to the work of God in you and allow Jesus to love you where you are. Ask the Holy Spirit to show you the wonder of His guidance and direction for your life. You'll never regret it.

The Rustle of the Trees

NIKI

AS I SIT IN MY COMFORTABLE "quiet time" chair every morning, I can see the leaves on the trees outside my window rustle in the wind. It so often makes me think of God as I contemplate the magnificence of His creation. I see blue sky, puffy white clouds, emerald green grass and leaves. At this time of year, there are daffodils swaying to a beat only they seem to hear. And the wind. I can see the result of the wind moving in the rustle of the leaves and the swaying of the flowers, but I can't see the wind itself.

Jesus used the wind as an analogy of a life lived through the guidance of the Holy Spirit. I can't see the Holy Spirit at work in me and in my life, but I can see the results of the Spirit moving through the continual changes in my heart. I can't see the future, where the Spirit is taking me. I can't even see the next step, but I know He is in me, and He is moving. Just like the wind.

Sanctification is the slow process of the Holy Spirit moving me toward becoming more like Jesus. It will take my entire lifetime. The Holy Spirit has His work cut out for Him! It's easy to become impatient with the process. Just as we learn to trust in God's timing in other things, though, we can learn to trust His timing in our sanctification. With trust, there comes peace and contentment right where we are.

All of us who have submitted our lives to Jesus will one day stand before God, carrying the perfection, righteousness, and holiness of Jesus Christ in our hearts—made whole, made new, and made perfect, just as God intended from the beginning. Thank You, Father, Son, and Holy Spirit.

Thank you, Father, for leading me in the way of the Spirit. Teach me the things you want me to know, and show me how to love You more. Amen.

Day 22

. . . as sorrowful, yet always rejoicing; as poor, yet making many rich; as having nothing, yet possessing everything.

—*2 Corinthians 6:10*

Have I Got a Gift for You!

NIKI

THIS VERSE IS A WONDERFUL summary of life following Jesus. No matter our circumstances, our innermost heart posture can be joy, because even if we lost everything (Job comes to mind), when we follow Jesus, we still have and always will possess all we truly need. Jesus gave us a gift no one or no circumstance can take from us—life with Him forever.

Even if we have nothing else to give, we have Jesus to give to others. God sent Jesus to us for our reconciliation with the Father, but also so we can share Him with someone else. Jesus is the greatest and most meaningful gift of all time!

Let me confess. I have a shelf in my bedroom closet where I keep gifts I've received that I plan to re-gift to someone else at some time in the future. Maybe you do, too.

We've all probably re-gifted something at some time in our lives. We often do it in shame, though, not wanting anyone to know we're giving a gift someone else gave to us. But re-gifting Jesus is a "go tell it on the mountain" moment! There is no shame in sharing with someone else the joy of an eternity with our God.

81

There's another significant difference in the spiritual re-gifting of Jesus and the re-gifting of those material things on my closet shelf. We re-gift because we don't want what someone gave us. But in sharing Jesus, we can know we're giving the greatest gift—the only one that has eternal value—and yet, we also get to keep Him for ourselves. Because of this miraculous nature of gifting Jesus to others, we can tell about our Jesus, crucified and resurrected, over and over again. There is no greater gift or privilege. Go tell the world!

Yet

CONSTANCE

IT'S THE WORD "YET" IN THIS Scripture that stands out to me. *Yet* always rejoicing (seriously?), *yet* making many rich (how?), *yet* possessing everything (really?). How can one do any of these things out of a life of sorrow, poverty, or emptiness?

Paul was aware of the deepening struggles of hardship, calamities, beatings, imprisonments, sleepless nights, and hunger the early church was experiencing; *nevertheless,* he knew there was a way to live with hope of what is to come even while in the now. We can know it, too. As servants of God with the power of the Holy Spirit within us, we can strive to widen our hearts to both experiences, suffering yet rejoicing, rich in His goodness, and possessing all we need for today. I witnessed this contrast while on a medical mission trip in Africa.

I saw desperately poor people walk miles each day to our clinic to receive treatment. They knew sorrow and pain as they watched their children and friends dying for lack of medical care. They struggled to make enough to support their families, yet they possessed a certain joy and fullness of life. I was humbled by their love, peaceful natures, and beautiful spirits. These Togolese men and women found the secret to being content in all things.

I share this story because there's a way of living in the midst of sorrow, pain, and "not yet" answered prayers. I see it in Jesus' life, the way He loved, His humility, the way He poured life into each person He encountered. Many who were sick, sorrowful, and poor rejoiced in the Messiah they had been waiting for. After an encounter with Jesus, everything changes. Nothing compares to knowing our Lord and Savior.

We can experience sorrow and times of lack, yet still know joy, wisdom, and abundant life—the entire mixed bag—when our hearts are filled with the love of God. He offers a way of living, of possessing everything that matters even in a world full of pain. May we always keep our eyes on the prize!

Dearest Father, help me find the fullness of joy in the love of Christ. Thank You for the privilege of sharing Your story with the world. Give me the words to draw people near to You. May I always embrace and possess all You have for me. Amen.

Day 23

But the midwives feared God, and did not do as the king of
Egypt commanded them, but let the male children live.

—*Exodus 1:17*

Do You Really Want Authority?

CONSTANCE

I HAVE MET MEN AND women who, like me, struggle with shyness
and insecurity. But we can display skill and expertise in our work
because there's a certain confidence that comes in staying focused
and determined regardless of our weaknesses. This self-confidence
supersedes the timidity. When I believe deeply and completely in
something, I am not deterred! The midwives in Exodus 1 exemplified
this same trait.

In a Bible story or passage, when people are given specific names,
there's usually a reason, and we should pause and take notice. The
midwives, Shiphrah and Puah, are mentioned only in Exodus 1—and
only once. Shiphrah's name means "does good," and Puah's name
means "to cry out." Some theologians suggest they may have been
mother and daughter midwives. I believe we know these two Hebrew
women's names because of what they did in order to further God's
purpose. They put God first, and they continued to bring new lives
into the world.

The king of Egypt issued a horrifying command to the midwives.
He wanted them to kill all the male Hebrew babies when born. His

reasoning was driven by fear, insecurity, and power. He was terrified the Hebrews were multiplying so greatly they would join the surrounding countries and overtake the Egyptians.

The midwives heard the king's command and went away from his presence, but their calling was to assist in bringing life into the world, not take it. So, they defied him. Later, the king summoned them and asked why they didn't do as he commanded. Their reason was the Hebrew women vigorously delivered their babies before the midwives arrived. Brilliant! But there was another reason, the real reason. The male babies lived because Shiphrah and Puah stayed true to their faith and feared God more than they feared the king. For eternity, they will be remembered for their courage and wisdom and their profound reverence for God and His laws. It wasn't the king of Egypt but the God of the universe they feared. The Hebrews continued to be fruitful and multiply, even in the face of the king's command.

Like these brave women, our heartfelt beliefs and love of God and His laws will guide our lives and keep us focused and determined to be true to what is right.

Fear or Fear?

NIKI

WHAT DO YOU THINK OF when you hear the word "fear"? I grew up in a church that preached the fear of God, teaching that God was someone to be afraid of, terrified even. Many times, I sat in a church pew with my elementary school class awaiting my turn to enter the confessional. As a second grader, I expected damnation instead of love, and that expectation grew into fear. I imagined how disappointed God was with me.

For many years, I didn't understand that for a Christ-follower, to fear God is to hold Him in the highest regard, to be in awe of His power, His majesty. It is a humble reverence of God. How my relationship with God changed when I came to understand the true meaning of the fear of God! This is the fear the midwives, Shiphrah and Puah, had for the Lord.

Their faith was grounded in their reverent fear of God and gave them courage to disregard Pharaoh's command to kill male babies born to Hebrew women. Pharaoh had the power to execute these midwives. Yet, even with the possibility of death, Shiphrah and Puah chose to follow the higher authority of the God they feared. Their reverent fear and faith in God moved them to obedience to God's commands instead of Pharaoh's. God's plan to grow the Hebrew nation would not be thwarted, for He is faithful to His promises.

God rewarded the midwives because they feared Him. He blessed them with families of their own. But because the midwives disobeyed Pharaoh's command, did they also lie to him when confronted? Did God overlook a lie, let a sin slide? Nowhere does Scripture say the midwives deceived Pharaoh. We can't assume they made up a story. The midwives could have ensured they arrived late to Hebrew births, or it could be true about Hebrew women, that they tended to deliver babies quickly, as the passage states. That scenario fits perfectly into God's plan to grow the Hebrew population. All we know for sure is what Scripture tells us.

Fear of God (reverent awe) leads to obedience, and God blesses obedience. May we always choose obedience because we fear God and refuse to fear the world. God opened the way for us to come directly before His throne of grace and mercy. I know now, when I come before Him with confession and repentance, to expect love and forgiveness.

Help me, Lord, to choose obedience, because of who You are and how You love me. May I always respond with reverence and awe to the wonder of Your greatness and love. Amen.

Day 24

"Nothing is covered up that will not be revealed, or hidden that will not be known."

—*Luke 12:2*

Can't Hide Forever

NIKI

WHEN I WAS THIRTY YEARS OLD, my kids and I spent the summer in Japan with Joe who was deployed there for six months. I don't remember how it came to be, but another Marine Corps wife and I were asked to be models in a fashion show for a Japanese department store. It was exciting and great fun, but what we didn't know ahead of time is we would be wearing Kabuki masks as we walked the runway. Kabuki masks have long existed in Japanese culture and are a symbol of traditional Japanese art. The masks we wore were wooden, painted white with small cutouts for eyes and nostrils and painted on lips. They completely covered our faces. With both of us having dark hair, we blended right in with the Japanese models. For the finale, all of the models came out onto the runway and only then did we remove our masks. There was an audible gasp when the crowd realized the two of us weren't Japanese but American!

While there was no harm in fooling the audience with masks on the runway, there is great harm in wearing religious masks. In Luke 12, Jesus specifically warns his disciples to be aware of the hypocrisy of the Pharisees. Their faith was more about show than it was about love. They proclaimed one thing and lived another. Authentic faith is a very big deal to Jesus.

The Message translation eloquently paraphrases the first couple of verses of Luke 12, "He said to them, 'Watch yourselves carefully so you don't get contaminated with Pharisee yeast, Pharisee phoniness. You can't keep your true self hidden forever; before long you'll be exposed. You can't hide behind a religious mask forever; sooner or later the mask will slip and your true face will be known.'"

Thankfully, authenticity isn't based on perfection. Lord knows we will never be perfect. Authenticity is about engaging with the Holy Spirit and allowing the process of heart change. Being genuine in our faith is living out for all to see what we proclaim to believe, being the same behind closed doors as we are in public. We're to be imitators of Jesus, and Jesus is all about love. He came to serve, not to be served.

There is no one better to emulate than Jesus. May we always be genuine in our faith, living a life of love and service to the best of our abilities. Not perfect, but authentic. May we walk the walk and not just talk the talk.

The Truth Revealer

CONSTANCE

AS A NEW CHRISTIAN ATTENDING a smaller non-denominational church with a wonderful teaching paster and a gifted music leader, I was happy and growing spiritually. The anointed worship leader led us for one hour into the presence of God every Sunday. It was as if we were worshiping at the throne of God. We knew something special was happening at our little church.

One evening, I received an email to attend an important meeting.

Once we gathered, one of the elders proceeded to inform us that there had been an affair between the pastor and his secretary and another between the pastor's wife and one of the youth group members. A collective gasp escaped our lips. Our hearts were crushed, our spirits grieving. We had been deceived, and three families were in distress. The grief was palpable that night and for weeks to come. Many left the church altogether, others chose a church with more safeguards, and some opted to stay. The ensuing weeks were hard, and I chose to leave the struggling church. My son needed a healthy youth group, and I needed a place to heal.

Deception is horrible when it happens in a small, close-knit church and particularly alarming when it involves a pastor or leader. Other hidden sins can be infidelity, manipulation, wrong teaching, anything that distorts the truth. Jesus was familiar with the dangers presenting during His ministry and warned the believers to be on watch. Deception could come, and it did, from the religious leaders of His day.

Though captured by Jesus' teachings, the Pharisees and Sadducees diligently tried to entrap Jesus in front of the crowds to persuade them not to follow Him. They seemed to be intrigued by Him and yet desperate to ridicule and prevent Him from teaching. Their own authority felt threatened by Jesus. But Jesus saw through the disguises of the Pharisees, the deception of the religious leaders, and the hypocrisy of their lives.

As painful as it was, God's mercy allowed the deception in our church for only so long. Jesus is the Truth Revealer. Trust Him. What is hidden or covered up will be made known. Why would we give any thought to living a life of deception when God sees it all?

Lord, give me a heart like Yours, filled with love.
Holy Spirit, let the light of Jesus shine brightly
through me for all the world to see. Amen.

Day 25

And he said, "My presence will go with
you, and I will give you rest."

—*Exodus 33:14*

The Sweet Presence of God

CONSTANCE

MOSES INQUIRED OF GOD as to who would be going along with
him and the Hebrews to the Promised Land. God responded, "My
presence will go with you." Moses, still seemingly concerned, replied,
"If you don't personally go with us, don't make us leave this place"
(Exodus 33:15 NLT).

I imagine God speaking those words to me. How comforting and
reassuring they would be when embracing any big change in my life.
We seek God's will and direction, but will His presence be there if
we miss His will?

A few years ago, Carroll and I sold our home in Mount Pleasant,
South Carolina to move closer to family in Tampa, Florida. We prayed
and believed the move was God's will and the right decision. So, we
stored sixty-five boxes and our furniture and went on a great adventure to find our new home. But we didn't! Two months in, Carroll
was having health concerns and wanted to go back to the doctors he
knew. We returned to South Carolina, and after six weeks of living
in a hotel, I secured an apartment. The next eight months were filled
with uncertainty and complete disruption. Our lives were turned

upside down, and I was disoriented. How did this happen? I thought we had heard God clearly.

That experience made me realize that God's presence is not the same as His will. But being in God's will makes being in His presence so much sweeter. Whether we get it right or miss the mark, God's work in us is always accomplished. Our *desire* to be in His will is what matters to God. Who we are becoming is what He cares about. His presence, I've learned, is with us always!

The presence of God enters the heart of surrender and trust. I needed to surrender my questioning of His will, our housing issues, health concerns, everything to Him. As I surrendered every single day, I experienced God's presence in the quiet dark of the night, sitting on my balcony, enveloped in His majesty and love for me. My dear friend, may you embark on your own personal journey of being in His presence.

God Uses Ordinary People

NIKI

MY OLDEST SON FOLLOWED in his father's footsteps and became an officer in the United States Marine Corps upon his college graduation. He was commissioned in August 2000, thirteen months before 9/11. He served three tours in Iraq and three in Afghanistan before leaving the Marine Corps thirteen years later.

On the first day of Operation Iraqi Freedom, he was in Kuwait awaiting the command to move out and cross the border into Iraq. After the bombing of Iraq began, the Iraqis retaliated by firing into Kuwait in the hopes of killing off their enemy before they even stepped foot into their country. I watched the start of the war on live TV like many other Americans. I remember sitting at my kitchen counter in utter shock, realizing my child, my firstborn baby, was being shot at and might possibly be killed. Fear gripped and paralyzed me. I couldn't go to work for a couple of days. When I finally forced myself to go to the office, I still couldn't function. I sat in my office holding back tears for several more days.

Finally, a coworker, a retired Marine Corps lieutenant colonel, came into my office, closed the door, and sat down in front of my desk. "Niki," he said, "this war could go on for a long time. I know that's hard to hear when your son is in it, but you have to find a way to be able to live with that fact. You can't go on as you have been." All I could do was cry as he left my office. It was a hard truth, but it snapped me out of the shock that held me. I can't say I immediately felt God's presence and His rest, but it was the first step. I decided to pray and try not to worry.

In Exodus 33, God tells Moses to take the people to the Promised Land. God also said He wouldn't go with them because they had turned away from Him, worshiping a golden calf while Moses was with the Lord receiving the Ten Commandments on Mount Sinai. Moses wanted to know who would go with him if God wasn't going. In response, God promised His presence and His rest to Moses.

Today, we have God's presence and the Holy Spirit who indwells those who belong to Jesus. His rest is always available through faith and trust in our good, good Father. Sometimes, the Spirit uses ordinary people to speak the truth we need to hear, truth that brings God's rest to our tortured hearts and spirits. I don't know if He used a retired Marine to speak the hard truth I needed to hear all those years ago, but I do know His presence was with me. And slowly, I surrendered my troubled heart to His rest.

Thank You, Lord, for the times you've ministered to my spirit in ways I couldn't even recognize. I long for Your presence and Your will. Lead me to Your place of rest as I seek Your guidance for my life each day. Amen.

Day 26

The Word Speaks

NIKI

ONE CHRISTMAS EVE, I STOOD between my youngest son and Joe at church services and sang my heart out. Soon, though, my mind wandered to how that scene was like heaven will be when we all will spend our time worshiping the Lord. The thought made me emotional, and it was suddenly hard to sing past the lump in my throat. As we sat down, I recovered my emotions and listened to what God had to say to me on that celebratory day.

We, as Christ followers, often pray to hear God's voice. But sometimes it's hard. The noise of the world and the distractions of the mind seem to flow in and out and all around in the space where we'd like God's voice to be. I can easily become envious of someone who says, "God told me . . . ." God's message is not often spoken in such a clear voice, and we can sometimes get hung up on wanting to hear God's voice audibly. I imagine it does happen for some, but I'm finishing up my seventh decade, and it hasn't happened for me.

Most often, God speaks to me through His Scriptures. That shouldn't surprise anyone, as speaking to us is the reason He breathed life into His Holy Word and inspired the writers to write what He wanted said. We who live in this "in-between time," after Christ's first coming and before His second, are blessed beyond measure to have the very words of God recorded for us. They are often His part of the conversation with us. Our part is to respond through prayer to what He speaks. Conversation goes in both directions.

God also sometimes speaks through others who know Him deeply and love Him fiercely. Look for divine appointments in your day, as you may be the receiver, or you may be the one through whom God speaks. I sometimes like to start my day asking God to give me His words and the opportunity to speak them to someone who needs to hear them. Then, I keep my eyes open.

On that Christmas Eve, though, as the preacher ended the service, praying for us and over us, I clearly heard God's Spirit speak to my spirit saying, *Jesus is the only Truth that really matters.* It jolted me because I knew it was God's voice in Spirit form speaking directly to my heart. The message was relevant to a prayer I'd been praying for over three years, asking God to make the truth known to someone who was determined to hurt my family with a vicious lie. It wasn't relevant to the sermon, but it was relevant to the state of my heart. God knows what we need, and sometimes, it comes when least expected.

Adorable Sheep With the Loving Shepherd

CONSTANCE

I'VE ALWAYS BEEN DRAWN to the faces of sheep. They're cute, for sure, and always smiling because their mouths are angled upward. I'm told these sweet animals experience a range of feelings because they are emotionally complex. They're gifted with wonderful vision and can see predators at a great distance; however, they're mostly defenseless, and when danger strikes, they run. Sheep are usually gentle and meek and affectionate with each other. Sheep provide food (meat, milk, cheese) and wool for us. Unfortunately, they are, as am I, frightened by sudden loud noises. They become agitated and difficult to handle. They (and I) need a Shepherd.

A Bible concordance will give you a plethora of Scripture references to *sheep* and *shepherd*. Jesus is called the Great Shepherd, and we're referred to as sheep. Why? Sheep have unique characteristics. They need a shepherd to lead and guide them, and they know his voice. They *want* to be shepherded.

Remember the beautiful example in Scripture of the one sheep that got away from the herd of ninety-nine. That one sheep was as important as the others to the shepherd. Jesus cares for and loves His sheep (His followers). He laid down His life for them (John 10:15). My friends, we are His people, the sheep of His pasture.

But what of His voice? Our unique voices are recognizable to others on phone calls or in a crowd. It's the sound, inflection, tone, or laughter that brings notice to us of a friend nearby. The same is true with our Lord. His voice can become a familiar voice in our lives.

Hearing His voice is of upmost importance in these times in which we find ourselves. Jesus wants us to hear and know His voice intimately and to follow Him, for in Him we live and breathe and have being. The Spirit is willing to show you, lead you, and give you peace.

Sovereign Father, thank You for knowing me and loving me as You do. Thank You for speaking to me, for allowing me to know Your voice. Help me to always follow, trust, and obey. Amen.

Day 27

*And they heard the sound of the Lord God walking
in the garden in the cool of the day . . . .*

—*Genesis 3:8a*

Where Are You?

CONSTANCE

THE CHOIR OF BIRDS WHISTLING their tune and the wind slipping through the trees, creating a symphony of intimacy with the Divine, makes nature my sacred place. I enjoy walking and praying in areas of natural beauty and ponds, forests, and mountains. Others may find their sacred place on the back porch or reclining in a cozy chair while the sun filters through the windows. Many find their favorite time to be with Jesus at the end of the day when all is done and the kiddos are sleeping.

God's intention has and always will be relationship with His creation, including us. He created the Garden of Eden, not only for Adam and Eve's enjoyment but also for His own. In this lush garden of extravagant beauty and provision, God desired a unique bond with His first humans. Can you imagine hearing the Creator's *familiar sound* walking in the garden? It was most likely a normal occurrence for Adam and Eve. But one day, something went terribly wrong. They disobeyed God, knew it, and hid from their Creator. Their beautiful union with God was broken. God then asks Adam, "Where are you?"

Certainly, God knew what had occurred between Adam and Eve,

but as with us, He asks us to go deeper into our story, to the root of our sin, to wrestle with our wrong choices and disobedience, to acknowledge what He always knows. God loves us and always wants the best for His children.

Perhaps He's inviting you for a walk in the garden, some time alone on your porch, or moments snuggled in your comfortable chair. What Adam and Eve lost we can have for ourselves. Are we in a place that encourages communion with the Lord, a quiet place away from distractions? Where is that special place for you?

He's inviting each of us into an everlasting friendship today, perhaps to explore; maybe to dance and sing praises with a joyful, grateful heart for Him; or just to be still.

I encourage you, dear ones, to engage your childlike wonder and curiosity. Be available for what your Father wants to give you.

"Wait 'Til Your Father Gets Home!"

NIKI

BEING BORN IN the 1950s, I grew up with a stay-at-home mom. I have five siblings, one of whom is a brother exactly one year older than me to the day. I love him dearly now, but when we were growing up, we fought *a lot*. I don't remember the details of most of our fights, but one day, in the midst of a battle, I threw a large, heavy harmonica at him. I missed my brother but hit the beautiful walnut cabinet of the only TV we owned. It left a gouge, a big one. It was then my mother said the dreaded words to me, "Wait 'til your father gets home!" Now, more than a half century later, I don't even remember my father coming home that day or what the consequences were. What I do remember was hiding in my room for the rest of that day, terrified at what might happen when my father did get home. He was a father to be feared.

Genesis 3 records the fall of mankind, the sin of Adam and Eve. The consequences of that sin are still unfolding today. That first sin changed everything except God's love for the man and woman He created. As God was walking in the garden, He already knew things had changed. Yet, He pursued them even in the shame of their sin. They heard Him but hid themselves.

I wonder if they feared God (not awe but genuine fear) in those moments of hiding the way I feared my father coming home that day. What Adam and Eve had yet to understand is that God loved them no matter what. Just the way He loves us today. "For I am sure that neither death nor life, nor angels nor rulers, nor things present nor things to come, nor powers, nor height nor depth, nor anything else in all creation, will be able to separate us from the love of God in Christ Jesus our Lord" (Romans 8:38).

God created us for relationship with Him. He pursued Adam and Eve even after their sin, and He pursues us today. His mercy, grace, love, and forgiveness know no bounds. May we not hide in shame but run to Him.

Father, thank You for loving me—no matter what. Invite me into Your garden to abide with You, to play, and to be. Amen.

Day 28

I have not hidden your deliverance within my heart; I have spoken of your faithfulness and your salvation; I have not concealed your steadfast love and your faithfulness from the great congregation.

—Psalm 40:10

None of Your Business!

NIKI

I GREW UP IN A CHURCH that didn't talk much about faith outside the doors of the sanctuary. It was a "Sunday morning" kind of faith. Never would I have thought about engaging someone in a conversation about God, whether it be a fellow churchgoer or someone outside the faith. My church upbringing led me to have thoughts contrary to David's about sharing my faith.

David wrote Psalm 40 and many other psalms. He didn't hide his faith like I did. He talked and wrote often of God's love and faithfulness. I had no clue sharing Jesus was a part of my faith walk. To me, my relationship with the Lord was private. It was between God and me, and none of anyone else's business. So not true!

A few years into my closer walk with the Lord, I heard a pastor say, "Your faith is personal, yes, but it's not private." It made me realize there's a big difference between personal and private. Yes, a relationship with Jesus is a deeply personal experience, but we're meant to share it. Christ Himself gave us the mission to spread the gospel to the ends of the earth. "Go therefore and make disciples of all nations, baptizing them in the name of the Father and of the Son and of the Holy Spirit" (Matthew 28:19). God's desire is that everyone should know Jesus, that all should be saved. How can they know Him if we don't talk about Him?

The miraculous thing is God doesn't leave us on our own, not ever. He equips us for our mission. The more we experience His unfathomable love, the more we will want to share what we know of Jesus and what He's done for and in us. It is deeply personal, but don't let it be private. Jesus changes everything. Let's tell the world!

Proclaim the Goodness of the Lord

CONSTANCE

WHEN I CAME TO FAITH in Jesus in the mid-1980s, my sins were forgiven, and I began a love relationship with Him. I was thrilled with my new identity and giddy with joy. My life was full and abundant, and I had a new beginning. I wanted to tell everyone about Jesus! I intentionally looked for people with whom to share my faith and my experience. I talked to the homeless, my Jewish boss, anyone who would listen about God and how He changed my life through Jesus Christ. I wanted people to know about my Father, Jesus, and the Holy Spirit.

The enemy would have us keep quiet about our faith and about our stories of deliverance. But we mustn't stay quiet! We might not be accepted at times, may be ridiculed, even mocked, but we must press through for the sake of humanity. I have experienced a plethora of reactions, but the message of Jesus is most important.

David's prayers of lament and praise to God in the psalms have been a blessing to me over the years. His vulnerability to pour out his anguish and frustrations or his "near death" experiences and yet, at the same time, his adoration for God, who delivered him through it all, is beautiful. His life was anything but perfect and his failures numerous, but his love for Yahweh, the Great I Am, is undeniable. David's freedom to share God's faithfulness in his life despite his weaknesses and failures is a perfect example for us.

The psalms articulate our hearts' deepest brokenness and ultimately deliver us to the grandeur of God. Our personal stories of deliverance, of transformation and renewal, can become the impetus to lead others to the steadfast love and faithfulness of the Almighty. Like with David, our stories can bring hope out of our pain—something our world desperately needs.

Not all struggles end with good results. Some endings are slow in coming or not at all visible. But our life experiences reveal the ongoing redemptive story of God in our lives. People want to see the evidence of God. Don't you?

I don't necessarily begin with the salvation story when I meet people, but I do tell stories, listen to those of others, share a nugget of trust, and offer a smile and hug, letting them know, "I see you." I don't conceal God, and I, hopefully, display Jesus. It's gratifying to represent Jesus to a lonely, sad, and suffering world. Try it!

Father, bless me with every provision I need to share Jesus in ways that will draw others to You and bear much Kingdom fruit. Amen.

Day 29

> *The Samaritan woman said to him, "How is it that you, a Jew, ask for a drink from me, a woman of Samaria?" (For Jews have no dealings with Samaritans.) . . . So the woman left her water jar and went away into town and said to the people, "Come, see a man who told me all that I ever did. Can this be the Christ?"*
>
> —John 4:9, 28–29

Thirsty for Living Water

CONSTANCE

IN MY MUCH YOUNGER YEARS, I would have placed myself as the Samaritan woman in this story, facing Jesus at the well, longing for a life of love, protection, and respect. Not that the men I met didn't care, but they couldn't love me the way I deeply desired. I struggled to prove I was worthy to be accepted by others, that I wasn't damaged by childhood sexual abuse. I wanted to love and be loved. However, I didn't know what love really was until I met the Man at the well.

The passage of the Samaritan woman at Jacob's well leaves us with much to ponder. Did she feel ostracized by the people of her village? Was she not loved the way she desired or should have been? Though they knew about her, did anyone really *know* her? I imagine she longed to be respected and appreciated and may have been bitter. Even though her life was not what she had hoped it to be, she came from a people and forefathers who had worshiped God on that mountain and drank water from Jacob's well.

The woman arrived at the well at noon where a thirsty and weary Jesus greets her, asking her for water. Surprised that a Jew was speaking to her, a Samaritan woman, she continues the puzzling conversation.

Jesus describes Himself as the giver of living water, forever satisfying one's thirst. She's curious; what is this living water? Jesus reveals elements of her life that are shameful for her, and she soon realizes He knows everything about her, her deepest secrets and sorrows. Could He be the Messiah for whom she has waited? Jesus responds, "I who speak to you am he." He embraces her vulnerability, and she sees herself forgiven, free, and loved. Leaving her empty jar for living water, she runs back to her village, proclaiming her encounter and asks, "Can this be the Christ?" She knows!

Jesus sees me, and He sees you. He receives us as is, no matter the current or past state of our lives. Receive Him now if you don't already know the fullness of our Lord.

Heavenly Encounters

NIKI

THIS SAMARITAN WOMAN KNEW HER reputation and what people thought of her. She knew the other women would draw their water from the well in the cooler parts of the day. Drawing her water at noon allowed her to isolate herself and avoid having to be around others who knew her story of multiple marriages and living with a man who wasn't her husband. There could have been shame in her countenance. She didn't expect to encounter anyone, much less a Jewish man who would speak to her.

Yet, speak to her, Jesus did. Jesus pursues all people, no matter who they are and what they've done. The fact she was a sinful

Samaritan woman had no bearing on God's love for her. God desires no one should be separated from Him and wants everyone to come to repentance.

The amazing part of this story is how the Samaritan woman was changed by her encounter with Jesus. She left her shame, along with her water jug, and ran back to the town—the very people she was hoping to avoid—to tell them about Jesus! It's still the same today. An encounter with Jesus changes us from the inside out.

A similar change happened to me in 2009. We moved to a new city and began attending a nondenominational community church for the first time. I encountered Jesus through a discipleship ministry of that church like I never had before. Through that ministry, I learned how to spend time with Jesus in His Word every day. My heart, mind, spirit, and soul were opened to hearing God speak personally to me. For the first time, I understood what a relationship with God meant. God wanted me to know Him deeply and intimately. Like the Samaritan woman, my encounter with Jesus changed me. Hers happened with hearing Jesus speak directly to her with His voice; mine happened with Jesus speaking personally to me through His written Word.

Jesus told the woman everything she had ever done, just as He knows everything I've ever done, and He still loves me. And like the Samaritan woman, I've left shame behind, and just like for her, God empowers me to tell the world about my Jesus. God's desire is still the same today—that none should perish and all should come to repentance and a relationship with Him. Don't wait another moment. Run to Jesus!

Lord Jesus, thank You for pursuing me when I didn't even know I needed You. Draw me near, Father, and help me to know You in ways I have yet to do. Amen.

Day 30

Then Moses turned to the Lord and said, "O Lord, why have
you done evil to this people? Why did you ever send me? For
since I came to Pharaoh to speak in your name, he has done evil
to this people, and you have not delivered your people at all."

—Exodus 5:22–23

Revel in the Unexpected!

NIKI

WHEN FOLLOWING GOD IN OBEDIENCE, suffering may persist, or even increase, as it did for the Israelites when Moses obeyed God's call to go to Pharaoh. Moses expected God to act in a certain way and to act *immediately.* We often expect the same. If I've learned anything through my years of walking with Jesus, it's this: God does His work in unexpected ways. I think He must love surprises. I do, too!

I once planned a getaway for Joe's fortieth birthday. After he left for work in the morning, I packed both of our bags, picked him up in a rented limousine at his office at the Pentagon, and whisked him away to the airport without giving him a clue as to where we were going. It brings me joy when I'm able to plan a sweet surprise for someone, and I can see they appreciate the love that went into planning, even the most insignificant items. I believe God might just get the same kind of joy in surprising us in how He works. When I get glimpses of God's hand at work in my life—to even the smallest of details—it leaves me awe-struck.

In those moments of awe, my mind is drawn back to the Lord's words in Isaiah 55:8–9: "For my thoughts are not your thoughts, neither are your ways my ways, declares the Lord. For as the heavens are higher than the earth, so are my ways higher than your ways and my thoughts than your thoughts." These are some of the most comforting words in all of Scripture. God doesn't expect us to understand His ways but to trust in His goodness and love for us.

The surprise I planned for Joe was completely unexpected. During the Exodus, Moses saw God move in some unexpected ways, too. His power and majesty likely left all of Israel with mouths agape in awe.

Finding Rest in the Wildness of God's Plan

CONSTANCE

HAVE YOU EVER GRUMBLED TO GOD about why something happened the way it did? Moses, a giant of the Christian faith, was confused, bewildered, and angry that God had yet to deliver Israel out of slavery. He wanted God to do it sooner and with retaliation for the pain and suffering the Israelites had endured. Moses doubted God's choice of sending him for this task in the first place.

We often ask God to fix this, do that, find this. To do it our way. But God has a plan for each of us that will be better than we can envision. There may be some hard seasons to go through before we see the fullness of His will in our lives. The question is, will we lose heart, forsake our Lord, seek after other gods, or fall for the enemy's trap as any number of people in the Bible did?

There were reasons why Pharaoh wouldn't let the slaves go for three days to worship their God in the wilderness. God's larger plan of deliverance from Egypt for the Hebrew slaves came ultimately through Pharaoh's hardened heart and reluctant refusal to let them go. It took ten plagues, and finally, Pharaoh met the God of the Hebrews. God's plan included Pharaoh's hardened heart. Imagine that!

I have lived long enough and experienced life as a child of God to have times of bewilderment, confusion, and disappointment in why things aren't happening the way or in the timing I'd hoped. Finding rest in the wildness of God's plan for our deliverance, a plan more detailed than we can possibly know, takes faith and trust. Remember the One who gives you breath to breathe, eternal life beyond these limited human years, and is a Comforter in times of stress. Jesus is a Friend when you need a caring mentor, a Savior when you can't save yourself. He is trustworthy and true, will never forsake you, and loves unconditionally. This is the One in whom we place our trust.

Most Holy Father, help me to wait for Your perfect plan to unfold. Thank You for giving me faith to accept I won't always understand all that You do. May I remain faithful, trust You, and rest in Your presence. Amen.

Day 31

His disciples did not understand these things at first. However, when Jesus was glorified, then they remembered that these things had been written about him and that they had been done to him.

—John 12:16

My Mama Said, "You'll See One Day . . ."

CONSTANCE

FOR THREE YEARS, JESUS AND his disciples walked the earth together. The relationship started when he invited them to follow Him. The twelve were the ones called to Jesus' inner circle. It didn't take long before the disciples concluded Jesus was the Promised One, the Messiah who would deliver the children of Israel from injustice and persecution, from the heavy-handed governments that forced their obedience.

The disciples were privy to the readings from the Torah scrolls and other manuscripts. They were fully aware of the prophecies foretelling of the coming Messiah. They feasted together and saw Jesus heal the sick, restore the blind and disabled, and deliver those oppressed by demons. They listened attentively as He taught and ministered to multitudes. The apostles were caught up in the moment, so to speak, engulfed totally in the life of Jesus.

Yet, somehow, they neglected to see their hero as a suffering servant, the One who came to rid the world of evil. The Scriptures prophesy both sides of Jesus in Isaiah 53 and 42:1–4. Sometimes, we forget we've heard the warning of future events until we're smack in the middle of them. Our minds receive information, but we aren't always ready to accept it. It was the same with Christ's first disciples.

My mother often said, "You'll see one day, when you reach my age." I thought it was hogwash. I wouldn't experience what she had. I was different; my life wasn't hers. Well, I'm the age now she was then. I can clearly see what she meant, and I find myself speaking her words to my own kids now. They often reject my wisdom, but I'm confident they'll remember and understand one day.

The words Jesus said to His disciples about His upcoming suffering and death came back to them later as they recalled all that had happened. Suddenly, the disciples saw what the plan was all along. It all made sense—Jesus' resurrection and return to heaven, His glorification, the renewal of all things for those who believed in Him. The apostles came to understand more clearly what Jesus was trying to tell them.

What is Jesus telling *you* today in Scripture?

I Don't Get It, Lord

NIKI

IN 2009, WE MOVED TO Dallas to live near our son, daughter-in-law, and first grandchild. I was over the moon with joy and excitement. Then, two short years later, my husband got word that if he wanted to keep his job, he would have to relocate to Charleston, South Carolina. I've always been excited about moving, but not this time.

However, I made up my mind to trust that God knew what He was doing. We sold our house and drove back to the east coast, with me wondering all the while why God would have answered my prayer to move to Dallas only to move us somewhere else just as I was relaxing into my role as "Mimi."

Now that we're back in Dallas once again, ten years later, I can look back and see God's hand in it all. I can see His purpose for our time in Charleston. In the moment, we often can't understand what God is doing, but in looking back, we can sometimes see what He was up to.

Those who were closest to Jesus—His inner circle of disciples—were no different than we are. There was much they didn't understand during Jesus' earthly ministry. They certainly didn't understand His torture and death when they expected Him to be their king who would deliver a kingdom to them in the Promised Land.

It was only when Jesus was raised from the dead and glorified that they were able to look back, ponder all that had happened, and begin to understand God's hand at work and His purpose for it all. It was true then, and still true now, that God works in mysterious ways.

So why did God take us to Charleston when my heart's desire was to be in Dallas? Charleston is where I met Constance! We've shared many adventures together, have had countless conversations about faith and our Jesus, and she has taught me the joy and beauty of deep friendship. Though I went to Charleston with a heavy heart, I returned to Dallas a decade later with the joy of my closest friendship in that very same heart. God is always up to something. May we trust to follow where He leads.

Thank You, Father, for knowing, better than I do,
just what I need. And thank You for sometimes
allowing me to see and understand it. Amen.

Day 32

"Hear, O Israel: The Lord our God, the Lord is one.
You shall love the Lord your God with all your heart
and with all your soul and with all your might."

—*Deuteronomy 6:4–5*

With Everything You've Got

NIKI

WHAT DO YOU THINK OF when you hear the word "might"? As a noun, the Merriam-Webster dictionary defines it as "the power, energy, or intensity of which one is capable." In other words, full out everything; all that you have within you. When Jesus was asked to name the greatest commandment, instead of might, He said, ". . . with all your heart and with all your soul and with all your mind" (Matthew 22:37), with *everything*.

Such succinct language doesn't leave much room for interpretation. God desires to be first in all areas of our lives. There is nothing too great to bring to Jesus, and just as important, there is nothing too small. If we desire to see God at work in the details of our lives, we need to cultivate the habit of bringing even the smallest of details to lay at His feet.

I've learned through experience that continual communication with the Lord is most natural when in a season of trial. When brought to the end of myself, there is nowhere else to turn but to Jesus. He is our sustainer. When coming out of a dark season recently, I committed to trying my best to continue the moment-by-moment communication with the Lord that had carried me through the suffering. My thoughts were never far from God. It can sometimes become more difficult, though, to even remember to talk to God when times are good. But, when God is *the* love of our lives, our thoughts will come back to Him again and again and again. Our conversation with Him never has to end.

In reality, this verse calls for a life of surrender. The dictionary defines surrender as "to give oneself up in the power of another." Sounds like the opposite of might, but to love God with all our might requires complete letting go of our control. God is sovereign over all things. He is worthy of our surrender, our praise, our worship, our *all.*

Leave nothing to chance; let's leave everything at the feet of Jesus and love Him with everything in us.

Love God Completely

CONSTANCE

I ONCE HAD DINNER WITH a ninety-nine-year-old Jewish man who served in World War II. Having experienced the gruesome war and the heinous Holocaust, he was agnostic, neither claiming faith nor disbelief in God. My heart grieved for Alan, and I acknowledged how impossible it is to understand the "why" of it all. Evil exists but so does good. How does one handle both good and evil in the world? To witness the worst of evil and the best of good, we must learn to hold them both and still believe.

As we talked, I recited, in Hebrew, this beautiful proclamation from Deuteronomy 6. I could sense a breakthrough in his thinking from the twinkle in his eye and the smile that creased his face. This passage, called the *Shema* in Hebrew, was spoken by the Jewish people in their worship and as they moved about the land. Moses received these words from God for the people of Israel, but Jesus also spoke them for the New Testament Church.

Living a life of loving God not only with our hearts, but also with our minds and bodies is the instruction. Loving God is a compass for living wholly before Him and sets our lives on a path of wellness. The New Living Translation states, "The Lord is our God, the Lord alone." God wants our devotion to Himself alone, forsaking all other gods we might be inclined to follow.

We love Him with our hearts, but what about our minds and bodies? Our minds want to debate, and our bodies have desires. Struggles arise when our thoughts roam away from what is beneficial for us. When we don't take our thoughts captive, soon we find ourselves in a place we didn't intend, wondering how we got there.

Loving God with all our strength means a body submitted to the desires of God, not to the physical desires that entice us daily—the habits, wants, and addictions drawing us away from what is beneficial for healthy living. Wholeheartedly loving God is the purpose He wants for each of His children.

God has and will guide us toward that which brings life not death. He is the giver of our days. Loving fully begins with communion with God and leads to loving our neighbors as ourselves. Jesus said to love God is the greatest commandment of all. May we surrender daily to the God who loves us wholly and completely.

Father, You are my sustainer. Help me to love
You above all and with all. Amen.

Day 33

Perceiving then that they were about to come and take him by force to make him king, Jesus withdrew again to the mountain by himself.

—John 6:15

Oops!

CONSTANCE

SOME DAYS, I FEEL LIKE I'm on a merry-go-round, and the wooden horse isn't going fast enough to complete my endless list of chores, tasks, and errands. Eventually, "something" nudges me to create change, usually in the form of mistakes that occur when I'm going too fast.

Like, one afternoon, when I drove up to the gas pump, and Carroll got out to fill the tank. After a few minutes, I assumed the tank was full when I saw him walking toward the convenience store to pay. To save time, I began driving toward the store. The manager and Carroll sprinted out, yelling at me to stop. I had yanked the hose out of the pump, dragging it while still attached to my car. I was in a hurry and wanted to be helpful; however, I wasn't paying attention.

That event has served as a reminder for me to slow down, breathe, and take time before rushing out to tackle my "to do" list. Oftentimes, our schedules are full of good things, like helping others. But taking time before each interaction to be still, take a deep breath, and say a quick prayer can impact lives, especially our own.

Our Scripture story comes after Jesus fed five thousand men, plus the women and children. After that miracle, the people believed the Prophet they had been waiting for was there before them, the promised One spoken of in the Scriptures. Jesus perceived what was about to happen next and withdrew to the mountain by Himself. He often withdrew to a quiet place and afterward came back to serve and minister. He spent time alone with the Father, so He knew what was necessary in each situation and for each person He encountered. Ministry to others is often an outflow from our times of silence in solitude with our Father—listening and receiving from the Spirit what is necessary for the present.

I wish I hadn't been in such a hurry that day at the gas pump. Most of the crazy situations we find ourselves in are a result of hurrying. Our culture pushes us to do more with less time and energy. We don't always need to be the rescuer in every situation. What we do always need is the Holy Spirit's guidance.

Unbounded Edges

NIKI

ON MY FIFTIETH BIRTHDAY, MY coworkers and I were gathered around the conference table enjoying lunch. The story came up about how I had surprised Joe on one of his birthdays by picking him up at work and whisking him away on a weekend trip. I had just finished saying Joe would never think of doing something like that for me, when in he walks. It was so unexpected, it left me speechless. I looked at my friends, mouth agape. They were all laughing, as they knew what was about to happen while I was complaining about Joe's lack of initiative in surprises! I shut off my computer, grabbed my purse, and off we went for a couple of days at a charming boutique hotel in the Virginia countryside.

Has someone you know well ever done something completely unexpected? Or, have you met someone new, and as you got to know that person, he or she turned out to be completely different than you thought? That's what the Jewish people discovered about Jesus. He was not the king they were anticipating. They expected to be set free from Roman authority and to have their own sovereign nation established with the Messiah as their physical king. Yet, Christ's mission was much more than the people could ask or imagine. He came to give eternal life to all of mankind, to set the people free, not from Roman rule but from an eternity apart from Him.

We sometimes have a "small" view of God, a limited view of who He is and what He does, and it can show up in our prayer life. If we pray without first thinking about the power and the majesty of the God to whom we pray, we may unintentionally put limits on what we ask and how we expect Him to answer. God is limitless, powerful, holy, and greater than any words can describe. We need to unbind the edges of our expectations of what God can do!

May we pray for God to answer our prayers in the way only He knows is needed. Let's open our minds to not only God's unlimited sovereignty and power but also His unbounded, immeasurable love for us.

Mighty God, do what only You can do! Show me Your way, help me to slow down and wait when necessary. Amen.

Day 34

It was I who knew you in the wilderness, in the land of drought.

—Hosea 13:5

In Times of Spiritual Wilderness . . .

NIKI

IN THE MONTHS AFTER I first experienced a deep, close, intimate relationship with God, I worried that I would wake up one day, and it would all be gone. I feared finding myself in a spiritual wilderness. I didn't yet know God's promises to never leave or abandon me, much less trust in them. I voiced my fears to a few others, but no one was able to reassure me in the way I needed. My worries were stealing my joy.

I've since come to realize we *do* go through seasons of spiritual wilderness or dryness. In those times, as much as I want to hear God and feel close to Him, I don't. As the Israelites wandered in the physical wilderness, they often felt a spiritual wilderness, too. They doubted; they complained. They even wanted to go back to slavery in Egypt. But it was never God who pulled away from them. He knew them in the wilderness; He was always close.

The same is true for us today. In spiritually dry seasons, we can trust it's not God who has pulled away. He promises His nearness always. In times of spiritual wilderness, we're the ones who've moved away from God. It usually happens so gradually, with such subtleness, we may not even realize it until, suddenly, we find ourselves far from God.

When you feel like you're wandering in the wilderness, when you miss the fullness and joy of God's presence, it's time to press in. Get quiet and alone with God. Open His Word, and ask Him to speak to you. God does speak. He spoke all of creation into existence, and He still speaks today. Try reading and then spending some time quietly meditating on what you've read. Make alone time with God a priority every day, and you will find Him again.

Over time, I discovered there was no need to worry. God is always waiting for me to draw near to Him. Once I'm His, I'm His forever.

Deserts Into Lush Beauty

CONSTANCE

WHEN I THINK OF WILDERNESS, I think of uncultivated and un-inhabited places—regions of neglect that are void of life, places of barrenness and little water. There have been times when I have felt like I was living in a wilderness, experiencing a drought in my soul even while living in the midst of plenty.

Life looks good on the outside, but my soul is dry. As I struggle to discern what it is I need, I give over to the hunt for satisfaction, for acceptance, for love. Perhaps a break from a difficult season to recalibrate or a re-introduction to the Holy One is in order. From the day of conception, a longing for love is placed within each of us. That longing is for God, for communion with Him, the God of abundance and life. I've noticed that my entire life has been in search for Him.

For the first three decades of my life, my spiritual experience was a combination of Jehovah's Witnesses and Mormonism, with time in between for searching other alternative spiritual practices. However, while living in Hawaii, Woody, who had attended the meeting the night before, invited me to a gathering being held by a visiting evangelist.

After a brief sermon, there was an invitation to receive Jesus as Lord of my life. I went forward and prayed, but I left feeling jealous and perturbed. I didn't get the exuberant joy I was looking for and others seemed to receive. Yet, weeks later, Sebastian and I attended a similar meeting. Again, we went forward to pray. The prayers were the same, but this time, my spirit was open and receptive to His wooing and my heart's yearning. It felt different, and it was!

The next morning, I awoke to a new day with a transformed heart and a deep desire to know Jesus as I never had before. Mine became an exchanged life—His life for mine, and my life lived for Him. My heart heard the beloved call, "Arise, my love, my beautiful one, and come away with me" (Song of Solomon 2:10). I was redeemed in dramatic ways from the land of drought, loneliness, and worthlessness. God saw me in the wilderness of my disoriented, counterfeit life and made me aware of the path where I can live in His presence and have fullness of joy forevermore.

It's been forty years since I gave my heart to God. I now rest in His mercy and grace. Don't give up on God; keep going to the altar, if necessary; or find a Christ-follower to talk with about Jesus, how much He loves you, and what He can do for you. God is the voice calling to you in the wilderness.

Father of Hope, lead me into the abundance of Your heart. Bring the dry places in my life to a lush garden along the river of life. Amen.

Day 35

And he is before all things, and in him all things hold together.
—Colossians 1:17

Hard Times Are Growth Times

CONSTANCE

SOME YEARS SEEM SO HARD! For me, 2022 was one of those. When it drew to a close, I yearned for the coming new year, excited that it would be better than the "nightmare year" just ending.

Then, one morning, a gentle sentence spoken by the Spirit was the catalyst in changing my downtrodden attitude to one of gratitude. I was encouraged to recall instances where God showed up in my life that year. I couldn't remember much joy, only the endless months of agony and grief. But I sat quietly and humbled myself to ask God to reveal those times. Suddenly, one by one, He began reminding me of instances throughout those months when Jesus was there.

There was Turner, who sat with me for hours in the hospital while Carroll was in surgery. My church family, small group, and girlfriends who loved and prayed for us throughout those eight months of continuous hospitalizations and rehabilitation. Sweet Laura, who used her organizational gift and took charge, moving boxes so I could have a clear space when I walked into my recently rented apartment. Traumatized by the responsibilities of setting up a new home and Carroll's illness, I couldn't figure anything out, but God sent angels in human bodies to encourage and nourish my soul.

One evening, while sitting on the sofa after a day at the hospital, I heard God whisper, "Those boxes aren't going anywhere until you start opening them." So began a journey each evening, opening two or three boxes, hanging pictures, and setting up my kitchen. I was suddenly motivated to do what I hadn't been able to even imagine.

It was a very intense year of uncertainty and confusion, but suddenly, I was made aware of the beautiful "God moments" that had occurred throughout the year. Jesus had held it all together for me. I had been transfixed on the nightmare year, but then I started to see clearly. It was one of the best years, a year of intense growth, a year full of extraordinary blessings and encounters with Jesus. It was also the year Niki and I began writing the book you hold in your hands!

Friends, hard times are growth times. Growth times are extremely important and expansive for us. What is hindering you from believing Jesus holds all things together?

Without Jesus, I Am Nothing

NIKI

SEVERAL YEARS AGO, WHEN I was writing my first book, my editor questioned one of my sentences. Out of all her edits, this one has stuck with me. My book was about healing and finding identity in something other than the trauma of my childhood. I had written, "Without Jesus, I am nothing." She questioned how I could write such a statement when I had spent my life trying to prove to myself that I wasn't defined by my childhood—that I *was* something and I *was* valuable. I wasn't mature enough in my faith at the time to explain it to someone who didn't believe in Jesus. I believed those words I wrote, but I was just beginning to figure them out myself. So I hit delete and wiped those words from the page.

Unlike me when I wrote that first book, Paul, in his letter to the Colossians, understood where his own value came from. He set out to prove the preeminence of Jesus. Jesus was then, and is now, the only way to reconciliation with the Father. Paul knew what Jesus did on the cross and what Jesus continues to do—"in him all things hold together." We have value because of Jesus. This one short verse explains in simple terms that Jesus is God. He is before all things. In other words, Jesus has always existed with the Father and the Spirit and was not created by the Father. And He sustains all things; nothing would continue to exist without Jesus holding it together and allowing it to exist. That includes us!

Close your eyes for a moment and inhale a long, slow, deep breath. Now, slowly exhale. That very breath is a gift from the God who loves you. Paul confirms in Colossians 1:16 that all things were created through Jesus and for Him. Created and sustained. Nothing would exist without Jesus. He is the only One.

Today, I regret deleting those words from my book because I understand the depth of truth in my statement. Without Jesus, I am nothing, and with Jesus, I have everything I will ever need, most especially, a glorious and righteous identity. Everything.

Lord God, Beloved Jesus, show me the times You have intervened in difficult situations for me, how You held all things together in hard seasons. Without You I am nothing. Amen.

Day 36

*Better is a handful of quietness than two
handfuls of toil and striving after wind.*

—*Ecclesiastes 4:6*

Why Her and Not Me?

NIKI

ONE OF THE DANGERS OF being a writer is the tendency to compare myself to other writers. The same probably happens in other occupations, but because writing is so much a process of sharing heart issues with the world, it can leave me feeling vulnerable. And so comparison creeps in. *She writes so much more eloquently than I do, or I'm a better writer, but look at her success. Why hasn't that happened for me?* On and on, my thoughts can seesaw when comparison rears its ugly head.

Trying to be someone else or write like someone else is like toiling hard yet striving after wind. God created each of us differently and gave us unique gifts. No two people think or experience emotions in the same way, so what those two people produce with their God-given gifts will never be the same. That's a good thing. God wants me to be me and use my gifts in the way He's wired me, and He wants you to do the same. Comparison of our gifts, our successes, our failures makes little sense in light of God creating each of us like no other.

Comparison can lead either to pride or to pity. Thinking oneself as better is prideful; despairing over inadequacy is self-pity. Neither one is a gift of the Spirit. Comparison can lead to discontent, envy, depression, jealousy. Spend some time scrolling through your social media feed, and you'll understand. Feeding on constant over-the-top highlights of other people can leave one feeling depressed over the mundane-seeming life of one's own.

The answer to the negativity of comparison is learning to be wholly satisfied with the gifts, the circumstances, the individuality God has given to each of us. It's about contentment. Paul suffered much during his life, yet he was still able to be content because he had Jesus. He had a relationship with Jesus that changed everything for him, including the lens through which he viewed the world. "... I have learned in whatever situation I am to be content. I know how to be brought low, and I know how to abound. In any and every circumstance, I have learned the secret of facing plenty and hunger, abundance and need. I can do all things through him who strengthens me" (Philippians 4:11–13).

Striving after wind, like comparison, never leads to contentment. May we instead use our gifts to the best of our abilities and all for God's glory.

Quietness and Peace Versus Toiling and Striving

CONSTANCE

WHEN I WAS IN MY twenties, I enjoyed the admiration and esteem that came from my job. I was self-reliant. I had travel opportunities, fine clothes, and beautiful furnishings for my first apartment in Baltimore. I was indoctrinated by a world that told me what I needed to become successful and be happy. Even when I married, we became *two* people striving for more—a bigger home, finer cars—and we were working harder. There's nothing wrong with striving to do your best, but if the results are stress, anxiety, and lack of fulfillment after giving it your all, does it really matter?

When a horrific fire in 2023 wiped out an entire town in four hours in Lahaina, Maui, my hometown for three years many decades ago, I was struck by how life can change so quickly. All the effort to accumulate the things we love and longed for can vanish in moments through natural or even family disasters. Everything is gone, and life is changed for those who have made Lahaina their home. The toil of striving has become the pain of survival and rebuilding. It's one day at a time, holding on to each other for strength and help. Suddenly, desperation changes our priorities and needs.

We need God in our pain and suffering to bring us through a life-sucking season. We need peace in our souls, the peace only Jesus can give. The world bombards us with commercialism and the need for more as the way to peace and contentment. But Jesus spoke about the peace He gives to us, and quietness opens the door for this peace to reign in our hearts.

Trade self-reliance for reliance on God. You'll enjoy a calmer, simpler, and more meaningful life. Trusting God is the way to living a beautiful life, but our eyes can become fixated on the world's definition of beauty and meaning. We *will* experience troubles, hardships, and disappointments, but the Peacemaker infuses us with faith and trust in Him, not the world. We have the power to choose wisely, especially when circumstances turn our lives upside down.

Let's be mindful that belongings are extraneous and temporary. Quietness and peace come from within—a state of being that can't be lost unless we allow the values of the world to overtake it.

Giver of Life, help me to keep my eyes fixed on You and not let them wander to compare with how You may have gifted others. I am grateful for the wisdom of Your Word and the clarity of my days. Grant me Your freely given gifts of peace, love, grace, and goodness. Amen.

Day 37

*You also, be patient. Establish your hearts, for
the coming of the Lord is at hand.*

—James 5:8

I Want It Now!

CONSTANCE

MANY MOONS AGO, WHEN I DESIRED something but couldn't afford it, I would put it on "lay away," making payments until it was finally mine. The wait produced anticipation and taught me budgeting and patience. Then, my first charge card arrived! I didn't need to be patient; I could charge it, have it on the spot, and pay later (sometimes much later) with added interest.

Waiting patiently for something we desire—the house to sell, the vacation to come, or the person to get well—is painfully difficult. We want it to happen now, and if it doesn't, then we try to make it happen.

I was more patient when I first came to faith; I prayed and believed for everything I needed. As a single mom, I didn't have money for extras. And God made Himself visible over and over again with provision of every kind and answered prayers. Now, I can obtain most things I need without prayer, and those I can't, I do pray and wait. It's a struggle to wait patiently. Being older with less years ahead, it appears I have more projects I want to accomplish and places to visit. I'm finding my limited years are producing an impatient gal. It's not fun to be patient, but waiting is teaching me to slow it down.

James, along with many of the followers of Jesus in the first century, expected the Lord's return was at hand. Generations since have expected and waited, and now many are longing for His return as we witness the signs of the times for ourselves. We anxiously anticipate the answer to the Lord's prayer, "Your kingdom come . . . on earth as it is in heaven" (Matthew 6:10). Will our generation be the one?

In the waiting and anticipation of the Lord's coming, James tells us to be patient and establish our hearts. Are we ready for that day? Are our hearts wholly after God? Are our actions and reactions, our lifestyles, in line with the life Jesus modeled for us? We will never have it all together. If we did, we wouldn't need Jesus. A heart desiring the things of God brings great delight to our Father. Practice patience while trusting His perfect timing for Christ's return. Establishing our heart posture with His is what we do in the waiting.

Ready or Not!

NIKI

OUR FAMILY ONCE SPENT A glorious week at the beach in an oceanfront cottage. The first evening, a storm came rolling in. The sky turned black and looked like nothing I'd ever seen. Picture a thick blackness; a thin layer of light, yellow-colored sky beneath; and finally, the water reflecting the oily darkness above. It was eerie. All along the beach, people came out onto their decks, overlooking the water to marvel at the sky. My eldest granddaughter, who was around five at the time, looked up into the sky and said, "Maybe Jesus is coming back!" We laughed and agreed, "It could be," but none of us truly believed that to be what was happening.

Later, I realized she could have been right. None of us know the day or the hour when Christ will return. Jesus wants us to be prepared. He told us He would return to gather all those who belong to Him. He expects us to be watching and waiting, even as we go about our everyday lives.

How do we get ready for Christ's return? How can we watch and wait and yet still live in these earthly bodies, in this worldly place? By keeping an eternal perspective. "And whatever you do, in word or deed, do everything in the name of the Lord Jesus, giving thanks to God the Father through him" (Colossians 3:17). May our words and deeds shine Christ's light to everyone we encounter.

Let's draw close to God. Get to know Him intimately through consistent time alone with Him. Cultivate our ears to be attuned to His voice. Hearing Him comes with practiced listening, and it requires stillness and quieting the mind.

Jesus is coming back. We don't know when, but we know He is. Let us be the ones who are ready, who are watching, who are waiting. I love that my granddaughter's thoughts ran first to Jesus when she saw the unexpected black sky over the ocean. It could be today!

Holy Father, help me to live with my eyes fixed on Jesus and with an eternal perspective in my heart. Help me to be ready and waiting. Come, Lord Jesus. Amen.

Day 38

*For thus said the Lord God, the Holy One of Israel, "In
returning and rest you shall be saved; in quietness and in
trust shall be your strength." But you were unwilling . . . .*

—Isaiah 30:15

Control or Surrender

NIKI

MANY YEARS AGO, WHILE ATTENDING a fourteen-week study
group for women survivors of childhood sexual abuse, one of the
early lessons focused on control. I got the sense from the discussion
that control was not a good thing. I remember asking, "What's wrong
with wanting to be in control?" I couldn't understand, because I had
a deep need to feel in control of everything in my life back then. I
eventually came to learn about surrender and God's control, which
gave me a freedom like none I'd ever known.

In Isaiah 30, the Israelites were in a similar struggle with control.
They were looking to Egypt to help them withstand a battle with
the Assyrians instead of looking to God. Relying on Egypt was
something they could do by using their own power. Relying on God
would require a faith the Israelites seemed to always labor to find.

In verse 15, God spells it out plainly. In returning to Him and
resting in His power, He would save them. In their quiet trust in
God, He would be their strength. Yet, they didn't have that kind of

faith and took things into their own hands. Their desire for control was greater than their faith in God.

Friend, I don't know where you are in your faith journey, but can you relate? I can. Having had no authority over my childhood and its trauma, my desire for control as an adult was greater than my faith in God for a big part of my life. Thankfully, God didn't leave me there in my rebellion, and He won't leave you there either. God is so merciful and gracious. He pursues, and He also leads, guides, and gives direction.

It may sound contradictory, but only in surrender to the Lord and His control is real freedom found. May we always rest in God and not in our own strength or anyone else's either.

The Conversation

CONSTANCE

DURING A SPIRITUAL FORMATION CLASS at church, our pastor asked, "What is God showing you this week?" and "How is He showing up in your lives?" Several mentioned personal experiences, and some spoke of breakthroughs in family situations, but for my friend, Betsy, God showed her a beautiful example of friendship with Him.

Betsy and her husband met over forty years ago. Their new and exciting relationship began with a simple conversation. In time, this continuing conversation led to marriage. In the midst of their life together, there have been careers, new friendships, and raising kiddos, followed by grandchildren. Of course, the harmony between them hasn't always been perfect, yet through difficult times, they trusted God. Now, in the latter season of life, God reminded Betsy that the conversation she and her husband started years ago is what He desires with us—transparency and curiosity layered with trust in both good and difficult seasons. It's a relationship of love that matures day by day. This bond with the Creator of the universe is an ongoing conversation that begins the day we meet Him.

God created us for relationship with Him and with each other. When we say "Yes, Jesus" to His invitation to follow Him, we're invited into fellowship with the Father, Son, and Holy Spirit. Our journey involves trusting and resting in Him, getting to know Jesus, and becoming like Him.

Yet, I tremble when God says, "But you were unwilling." Why are we reluctant or ambivalent to draw close to Him? Distractions and stimulation overload can keep our brains in constant motion. But we're invited to the communion table, to intimacy with God, especially in seasons of trouble. My practice is to wait and listen quietly to what God wants to say to me. It takes discipline, but His strength awaits us. Let's make room for the conversation. God is always present and waiting.

Show me, God, how to find rest in the quietness. May the silence where I hear Your voice become louder than the chatter in my head. Help me to trust You, and may I be willing to obey always when You speak. Amen.

Day 39

"Therefore, I tell you, do not be anxious about your life . . . . Is not life more than food, and the body more than clothing?"

—Matthew 6:25

Living in a Bed and Breakfast

CONSTANCE

AFTER SELLING OUR HOME IN 1999 and waiting for settlement on a new one, Carroll and I lived in a bed and breakfast. Our room had a queen-sized bed, small dresser, closet, and bathroom. We each brought one suitcase and a toiletry bag, and contemplated how we would get by on less. It's not always easy to leave our comfortable homes and everything dear to us.

But soon, the simplicity of life embraced us. We lived like we were on vacation. Each morning, we were fed a home-cooked breakfast before work, and our evenings were spent paddling a canoe around the creek or reading a book in the gazebo while watching a sunset. Our evening meals were easy—takeout or a café, with the occasional meal at a friend's or family's home.

While our belongings were in storage, we had no responsibilities and the freedom to do whatever we wanted. Knowing we would be settling in our new home in a month was also reassuring. This kind of living would probably never happen again, so we enjoyed it. It was a life-giving experience, which included solitude and rest, play and refreshment, all while still working. Perhaps we might get bored of this lifestyle over time, but it certainly was a less stressful way to live. And we discovered four weeks wasn't long enough to become bored!

Jesus used His Sermon on the Mount to tell us how we're to live. Our verse for today falls under the subtitle, "Do Not Be Anxious." How often are we anxious about what to eat, what to wear, or what tomorrow will bring? Jesus said, in essence, why worry? The Father knows our needs, so seek Him first, and He'll take care of everything else. The emphasis is always on trusting and seeking God first.

It felt a bit unsettling at first when our living conditions were reduced to one room with limited resources, but Jesus reminds us to trust the Provider *for and in* all things and not to be anxious about our lives. God takes perfect care of the entire universe. Why wouldn't He take good care of us, too?

Naked Anxiety

NIKI

HAVE YOU EVER WONDERED ABOUT the purpose of dreams? What about recurring dreams? There are a lot of theories, some psychological and some superstitious. I've had a recurrent dream throughout my life. In the dream, for some unexplained reason, I find myself in a situation not wearing any clothes—stark naked. At first, I don't seem to mind, but as the dream goes on, I become more embarrassed as I wind up in the company of many different people. Finally, I try to find anything to cover myself, at which point I wake up. What's even more strange is no one ever says anything about me being naked. The only person who seems to care or even notice is me. I have to wonder what that's all about!

Regardless of the embarrassment in my dream, I know life is more than clothing and more than providing nourishment for our bodies. God created Adam and Eve without clothing, and they carried no shame. When sin entered the world, it brought a need to cover ourselves. And it was Jesus entering our world—dying and rising from the grave—that gave us the Bread of Life and the clothing of His own righteousness. It's because of God's grace and mercy that we're fed and clothed through the body and blood of Jesus. Freely given, ours to accept or reject.

If God never gave us another thing, He's already given us more than we deserve and the only thing we'll ever need—salvation in Jesus Christ. Yet, God knows our humanity; He knows our weaknesses; He knows and promises to meet our physical needs. My recurring dream often leaves me feeling anxious when I awaken until my thoughts come back to Jesus. Trusting God's provision is a powerful antidote to anxiety. God cares; God promises; God is faithful.

Faithful Father, thank You for Your provision for my every need, most especially for my greatest need. Thank You for clothing me in the righteousness of Jesus. Amen.

Day 40

There is a way that seems right to a man,
but its end is the way to death.

—Proverbs 14:12

We Don't Always Know Best, Even If We Think We Do

NIKI

FOR MY TENTH BIRTHDAY, MY parents bought me a new bicycle. It was a three-speed, and I'd never seen such a beautiful machine! My mother warned me, having never ridden a bike with hand brakes, I should start slowly and stay close to home. But soon after, my eleven-year-old brother and I decided to ride our bikes to our grandparents' house about a mile and a half away. All went well on the outbound journey. On the return, we decided on a different route, down a very steep hill. It wasn't long before my front wheel began to shimmy and shake as I tried to regain control of my bike. Panic gripped me. Not knowing what else to do, I squeezed hard on one of the brake levers. It was the front brake, and over the handlebars I flew, smack on my face and my mouth full of now-mangled braces.

Like my ten-year-old self, we all have a natural tendency to want to go our own way, despite having such limited knowledge when compared to our all-knowing God. There are ways that seem right to us but, in the end, at best, will leave us face-planted in the middle of the road. At worst, they lead to *eternal* death. Thankfully, God doesn't leave us to figure things out on our own.

One great source of guidance is God's Truth, His God-breathed Word to us in Scripture. His Word gives us the Way, the Truth, and the Life. Scripture helps us to discern right from wrong and equips us to follow God into fulfilling His purpose for us. God's Word also helps us to see, through the example of others, how some choices might turn out. He gives us what we need to know so we can avoid those poor choices.

God guides us when we ask Him in prayer. If you need wisdom in making a decision or choosing a path, ask God. He promises to give wisdom generously. God has also graciously given us the Holy Spirit, who indwells those who follow Christ. The Holy Spirit's "job" is direction and guidance.

God knows we need counsel, just like my mother knew in warning me when I got my new bike. May we be more open to guidance, direction, and correction than I was at ten years old, when I thought I knew better. The Lord knows best.

Trust the One Who Knows

CONSTANCE

SEVERAL YEARS BACK, MY COUSIN and I traveled to Ireland for a holiday. Excited, we grabbed our luggage and headed to the car rental kiosk. Soon, with keys in hand, we were directed to the location of our car. To our surprise, we were given a tiny car, which neither of us wanted. Back to the kiosk we went, where I insisted on a larger car with more space and comfort. The gentleman strongly suggested we stick with the tiny car, but I wouldn't have it. With our luggage in the trunk of a larger rental car, off we drove. Right away, I found myself challenged by not only driving on the opposite side of the road with a steering wheel on the opposite side of the car but also on the narrow two-lane, no-shoulder country roads. Traffic circles were even more interesting to navigate!

It didn't take long to realize that what seemed right to us before we hit the road was definitely wrong. We could die! By the end of our trip, our car had lost a mirror, and the fender was hanging off on the passenger side, plus there were a few other scratches and dents. When the rental car guy saw the vehicle, he jokingly said, "Aren't you glad you took total coverage?" We replied with a smile, "Yes, indeed."

We had not listened to a wise man, who knew exactly what we needed. I had to do it my way, which led to a damaged car and some serious stress. Praise God, we were safe on those narrow roads.

God has a plan for our lives and instructions for how best to live out our days. We tend, though, to sometimes ignore those commandments and the wisdom God has lovingly set out for us, following instead a path that may seem less confusing and more gleeful in the moment. We can play hard and make wrong choices, only to realize our mistakes later when we're in a dark place, and life isn't working so well for us.

Following God's direction, we have life eternal. Jesus said lay down your life and follow Me (Luke 9:23), receive Me as your Savior and Lord, and walk in the way of Light not darkness. He sets the way before us, and we walk in it . . . if we trust Him.

Sadly, many of us continue living recklessly as if we will never die. It seems right to us. However, we'll find, in the end, that kind of self-reliant life leads to eternal death. God yearns for us! Let's open our hearts to Jesus, choose His path, and walk in it.

Abba Father, show me the way everlasting; I desperately want to walk in it. I acknowledge You as my Savior. Teach me Your ways, Your path. Amen.

Day 41

. . . bearing with one another and, if one has a complaint against another, forgiving each other; as the Lord has forgiven you, so you also must forgive.

—Colossians 3:13

The Journey of Forgiveness

CONSTANCE

FORGIVENESS IS A BEAUTIFUL WORD. It evokes a feeling of humility and reunion in me. Forgiving one another is a life-giving action of the will and heart. Yet, forgiveness can be difficult to give and, at times, challenging to receive.

During Jesus' ministry, He offered forgiveness to many by saying, "Your sins are forgiven." Even while He hung on the cross between two criminals, He granted forgiveness to the one who acknowledged Him as Messiah and to the very ones who crucified Him. "Father, forgive them, for they know not what they do" (Luke 23:34).

Christ modeled forgiveness throughout the Gospels. The Son of Man understood human weakness, failure, and the struggles we would face. He understood our need for forgiveness not only from Him but also from and for each other.

Today, many hearts are wounded as we see the world divided, relationships among families and friends torn, and division occurring in almost every aspect of society. More than ever before, we need to consider how to repair our relationships through forgiveness. Not everyone will be accepting, but we do our part and God will do His. Some relationships may not give us the opportunity again.

Woody and I had many difficult times in our marriage, causing us heartache and suffering, which led to separation and divorce. It wasn't our intention to cause each other pain, but we did. Sitting on the sofa, in a conversation I remember well, we found our eyes deeply entrenched in each other's expression. Suddenly, he said with tears, "I see in your eyes the pain I've caused you, and I'm deeply sorry. Please, can you forgive me?" We cried and hugged and made our peace. We accepted the gift God gave us that night. Forgiveness was offered and received because God allowed this moment in our lives to be vulnerable and humble and open for repentance and forgiveness. It meant so much to us both but especially to me. That hard, moving conversation was the last time we saw each other, as he was relocating to Kansas the following week. Four weeks later, he suffered a severe head injury while being assaulted and passed away unexpectedly.

Let's do our best to walk with forgiveness and mercy for those around us. Time is precious and not guaranteed. We never know what God wants to do through us and for us when our hearts are open to His leading.

"Forgive Us . . . As We Also Have Forgiven . . ."

NIKI

MY HEART CARRIED A HURT for decades, many decades. The offense felt unforgivable. Then, I came to know Jesus just as I was beginning to work through the trauma and pain of my childhood.

Forgiving the one who hurt me still felt impossible, but when I read Colossians 3:13, I realized forgiveness isn't an option God gives us. It's a command. But that still didn't make it easy.

One of the most important things I've come to know over many years of walking closely with Jesus and healing from my trauma is that forgiveness has absolutely nothing to do with the person who hurt you. It's only about you and your heart. There's a famous quote about holding onto unforgiveness, which is attributed to many different people, "Unforgiveness is like drinking poison yourself and waiting for the other person to die." By holding onto bitterness, anger, and hate, you convince yourself you're hurting the one who hurt you, but it's not true. The only one who hurts is you.

Forgiveness is a process where you give your anger and pain to the Lord every time it rises up in you. Over and over again, no matter how many times or how long it takes. My process took years, but I knew I had truly forgiven when I could pray for good things for the one who hurt me—and mean it.

Forgiveness is also a mindset or, rather, a heart set. As I write, my family and I are walking a terribly dark road. We've been on this road for more than three years. This season is the hardest trial and deepest pain of my life because it hits me in my mama-heart. Nothing hurts a mom like seeing her child in unbearable pain and being powerless to stop it. The trauma may not be the same as I experienced as a child, but the process of forgiveness is. I've already forgiven the ones who continue to hurt us. In my heart, I know our enemy is Satan, and so I can forgive the ones he is using.

Father, soften my heart and give me all I need to forgive those who hurt me, just as You forgive me my sins and failures. Amen.

Day 42

When you give it to them, they gather it up; when you open your hand, they are filled with good things.

—*Psalm 104:28*

Mind Blown!

NIKI

THE OTHER DAY, I TRIED to find a particular verse to use in support of a devotional entry I was writing. I couldn't recall the exact wording or where it was located in Scripture. I searched my Bible app and Google, using the words I thought were in the verse. I wound up using a similar verse, but I knew it wasn't the perfect one.

At the start of my daily time with Jesus, I usually look at Facebook to read a devotional from an author I follow. The morning after I searched endlessly for that particular verse, I opened Facebook, and the post at the top of my feed—the first thing I saw—was a graphic written in beautiful script with the verse I had searched for! My jaw dropped in awe of God. It was such a small thing in the grand scheme of life, but God knew what I needed and surprised me by providing it.

God is always at work in our lives and in our circumstances. So often He works behind the scenes of our physical reality, and we don't see evidence of what He's doing. There are times, though, when God pulls back the curtain and gives us glimpses into His goodness and His hand at work. Our faith is thereby bolstered with a generous serving of joy, and our hope is replenished.

The morning He gave me the Scripture was one of those moments. He opened His hand before my eyes, and I saw it was filled with good things. I love when He does that! I don't ever want to forget how I felt when my eyes landed on that elusive verse that morning. Amazement, joy, awe—everything good. God not only knows all of the details of our lives, but He cares about every one of them. Contemplate that truth for a moment, and let God blow your mind with His goodness.

You Are Worthy, My Friend!

CONSTANCE

GOD IS EXTRAORDINARILY CREATIVE AND generous. He ordered into existence the world and its inhabitants. Proof of God's extravagant beauty is everywhere we go. I'm in awe of His kindness and love toward us. His bountiful forgiveness and restoration are offered to all who have been made in His image.

The writer of Psalm 104 beautifully pens a list of God's universal creativity. It's displayed in the sky and earth and sea for the entire world to enjoy and freely given to us to gather up. When I'm outside in nature, I'm flooded with extravagant wonder. Wildlife seems to mimic humanity in their way of cuddling their young; flowers pop up after a long, cold winter; and trees bring forth colorful greens. The birds sing. Looking up to the night sky, I'm speechless over what surrounds me. The glory of God is everywhere. We gather up these gifts, yet oftentimes neglect to thank the Creator for the miraculous blessings bestowed to us.

Even with all that, God still has more for us. I believe He opens His hand to disburse abundant and bountiful gifts, beyond the universal gifts of creation, to those of us who receive His sacrificial love through His personal gift of Jesus, His beloved Son. He offers gifts of compassion for the forgotten, an ability to forgive those who sin against us, power to love others, and joy in a dark world. These *good things* are gifts of grace to us for others. He wants us to have an open hand, not a closed fist.

Jesus gave us an example to live by. It's not easy; however, I'm confident God enables us to do the impossible as our hearts wholly seek after Him. I want everything God wants to give me. I'm sure you do, too. Gather it up from His open hand.

Awesome Creator, please help me to see what I don't readily see, to worship You with gladness and praise every day of my life. You are my Beloved, and I am Yours. Amen.

Day 43

> *And God said, "Let there be light," and there was light. And God saw that the light was good. And God separated the light from the darkness.*
>
> *—Genesis 1:3–4*

One Lit Wick

CONSTANCE

THIS EVENING, THE FULL MOON on its way up met the waning sun on its way down on opposing sides of the sky. The multitude of stars took a back seat to the moon tonight because of its brightness, but the stars will certainly have their moment of glory when the sky is darkened from a new moon. Light and darkness govern our lives, but there will always be a light in the dark sky.

Creator God spoke light into being on the first day of creation, separating the light from the darkness. On day four, God spoke into existence the sun, moon, and stars in the heavens. He proclaimed those lights to be signs for seasons, for days, and for years. But there is another Light and a different darkness, the darkness of evil. John spoke of Jesus as the Light of the world, the true Light who gives light to everyone. Those who choose to follow Him will not walk in darkness. We, who belong to Jesus, are to be lights shining brightly in this dark, imperfect, yet beautiful world.

On a recent trip to Israel, our guide led us deep into a cave in the wilderness. When we were seated, he requested we blow out our lit lamps. One by one, the room darkened, and then it was black—not a speck of light! I have never experienced the dark as I did that day. He lit an olive-oil-soaked wick in a small pottery lamp and placed it in a cubbyhole. The cave brightened and was soon flooded by the glow of the lamp. It was startling to see the darkness flee with just one lit wick. One small lamp of light can bring great clarity in the dark.

We are light bearers in this world. Jesus' intention is to draw all peoples to a relationship with God, and He wants to do it through us. Certainly, there is darkness in the world that wants to distract us, but the darkness won't overcome the Light of life in us. God is Light, and He indwells His sons and daughters.

Let your light shine. Don't be intimidated by the darkness. Even the softest of lights banishes the dark.

Let There Be Light

NIKI

THE HOUSE WHERE I GREW up was on a street that, once past my house, turned into a bridge over train tracks. The neighborhood kids made up scary stories about people living under the bridge and creeping up to the street from the tracks. I had to walk that street every day to get home but knew to stop at my house before the bridge. We weren't allowed over the bridge. In the daylight, I had no fear in walking home. At night, it was a different story. My mind would conjure up all kinds of threats, and I would find myself breathing quickly while hurrying to get to our door. Nothing ever happened to me on that street, but the dark felt unsafe and scary.

There's something about light that makes us feel safe. I have three grandchildren who sometimes spend the night with us. Inevitably, as we're tucking the two youngest into bed, they ask for nightlights and want them plugged into the outlets closest to their beds. They want the light nearby. It brings a sense of security.

Maybe you've gone to bed feeling anxious and worried about something only to wake up to the light of the next morning feeling surprisingly better about the situation just because of the light of day.

God created us with a need for light, and it never leaves us. It's evident in young children who need a nightlight to sleep or kids afraid to walk down a dark street. The true fulfillment of that need is Jesus. Until He returns and brings His Light, we have the lamp of His Word to light our way and draw us near to Him.

God provided the light for us in the beginning at creation. He brought the Light of the world to us in the incarnation of Jesus. He sustains us in this dark world by the light of His Word. He promises eternal Light in heaven for us through the glory of His Son. Though darkness may seem to prevail in this world today, darkness doesn't win. We have God's Light. Let's go forth and let it shine through us into a desperately dark world.

Dearest Father, refresh my spirit, soul, and body with life and light that I may walk in the way of righteousness and truth. I love you, Jesus! Amen.

Day 44

*"Can a man hide himself in secret places so that
I cannot see him?" declares the Lord. "Do I not
fill heaven and earth?" declares the Lord.*

—*Jeremiah 23:24*

How Big Is the God You Worship?

NIKI

JOE DRIVES A TWENTY-TWO-YEAR-OLD Toyota Camry. When it was new, it was the car I drove. One morning, I decided to parallel park the car on the street in front of the parking lot at my office because it was, oh, maybe ten feet closer to the building. On my first attempt, I realized the left side of my shiny new car was too close to the traffic in the street. I tried again. This time, I heard a gut-wrenching scraping sound as I backed into the spot. I quickly pulled out and decided to park in the lot after all.

With a heavy pit in my stomach, I walked around the back of my car to see bright yellow streaks of paint on the shiny silver fender. I had scraped thick yellow concrete posts that separated the lot from the street. The pit in my stomach became a lump in my throat as I thought about what to do. Could I somehow hide what happened?

A wet rag and an hour of elbow grease made my fender look almost new, except for a few scratches. Joe never knew what I had done to save myself ten steps that morning. I may have hidden it from him, but God knew.

152

God is everywhere, all at once, and He knows everything. It's scary or comforting, depending on whether you're trying to hide something. In Jeremiah 23, God warned his people against false prophets. Though they claimed to speak for God, they underestimated His Deity and Divine powers. They thought and spoke of the One True God as they thought of the other gods of whom they spoke—limited, with short-sighted awareness. God warned His people with a declaration of His omniscience and omnipresence.

I was nervous that day, as I drove home from work. Would what I'd done be found out? Though it never was, I needn't have feared. Joe would have taken it in stride and not held it against me. Even if we're nervous about taking our failures to the Lord, we can take comfort in knowing how much He loves us and knowing His forgiveness is infinite. We can be confident that our circumstances, to the smallest detail, hidden or not, are in His hands and in His heart. He is for us; there's no need to hide.

A Surge of Guilty Adrenaline

CONSTANCE

ONE MORNING, WHILE MAKING BREAKFAST, I reached into the freezer to retrieve two slices of bread. Noticing a half-eaten raspberry chocolate chip yogurt bar, I grabbed it along with the bread. Filling my mouth with the delicious taste of cold raspberry and chocolate, I turned around and came face to face with Carroll, who had been watching the entire time. A surge of guilt ran down my spine until we burst into laughter.

This silly example demonstrates that oftentimes we think we're hiding, only to learn that others see us—especially God. Perhaps we think God isn't interested in what we're doing because He's busy running the universe.

Our awareness of God's omniscience brings accountability to our actions, decisions, thoughts, and to how we treat those around us. Remember, "no creature is hidden from his sight, but all are naked and exposed to the eyes of him to whom we must give account" (Hebrews 4:13).

Even in our ignorance, doubts, and weaknesses, we're seen and known by God and fully forgiven through Jesus' blood on the cross. Nothing occurs without His knowing, not even sneaking a frozen dessert bar before breakfast! I smile when the Lord says, "Can a man hide himself in secret places so that I cannot see him?" Of course not. Remember, Adam and Eve attempted to hide from God after they sinned. He not only found them, but in His compassion, He clothed them.

All-Knowing Lord, help me rest in Your Deity. You see and know it all. Help me, also, to confess what needs confessing. Amen.

Day 45

And they prayed and said, "You, Lord, know the hearts of all, show which one of these two you have chosen to take the place in this ministry and apostleship from which Judas turned aside to go to his own place." And they cast lots for them, and the lot fell on Matthias, and he was numbered with the eleven apostles.

—Acts 1:24–26

Rock, Paper, Scissors

CONSTANCE

DO YOU HAVE TROUBLE MAKING decisions even though you've prayed earnestly about them? You always want to be sure your decision is the right one. In times past, when I wasn't certain, I would toss a coin. If I felt happy with how the coin landed, then it was over. However, if I was unhappy with the way the toss went, I would choose the opposite outcome because I didn't like what the coin toss chose!

The childhood game "Rock, Paper, Scissors" is similar. It's not unusual to resort to trying different ways to confirm a decision, but that doesn't mean we know what's best for us. We often push for a specific answer, no matter what. But the disciples chose a different way. They wanted God's best and believed He would provide when they cast lots to decide on Judas' replacement.

To fulfill Scripture (Psalm 109:8), the apostles needed to select a replacement for Judas, the betrayer. It was important the person chosen had been a witness to Jesus' resurrection. Barsabbas and Matthias were selected, but only one was needed. The apostles prayed together and then cast lots. Casting lots left the outcome to God, and Matthias was chosen. Does it show weakness to cast lots? I don't believe so. Casting lots was a common practice in biblical times. I think it shows reliance on God to provide the answer.

A wonderful verse in Proverbs 16:9 says, "The heart of man plans his way, but the Lord establishes his steps." In essence, God is in control, and whatever my plans may be, ultimately, God's will for me will come to be. Upon surrendering our lives to Jesus, we have the Holy Spirit within us to help comfort and guide us. We pray, we believe, and we trust that His will for us will unfold.

I wish we could be one hundred percent sure we hear God correctly. But seeking His will is what's most important. God knows what we desire and sees our hearts' motives. We must leave the rest up to Him and trust the result. Tuning into the Spirit of God is something we can rely on for the rest of our lives. There's nothing better for us. Drawing on the Holy Spirit's wisdom takes practice. Don't give up!

No Second-Guessing

NIKI

ABOUT FIFTEEN YEARS AGO, I was in a meeting with several women who led a church ministry. I was still a baby (maybe toddler) Christian. In the course of conversation, one woman, a single mom, told us she was selling her home. I didn't know anything about the home except that she said she had purchased it several years earlier without praying and asking God into the decision-making. Her comment stopped me in my tracks. At the time, I did pray, but I didn't even think to ask God to guide my decisions. And here she was selling her home because she felt it hadn't been the right decision to buy it, especially since God had no input. Her story changed how I made decisions from that day forward.

I began to pray over my decisions, yet I still found myself often second-guessing them. That is, until this story in Acts 1 changed my perspective yet again.

The apostles met to decide on a replacement for Judas, who betrayed Jesus and later took his own life. They had two men in mind, Barsabbas and Matthias. They prayed and asked God to show them which one *He* had chosen. They cast lots (rolled the dice) and chose Matthias. There was no second-guessing. The apostles had asked God for His guidance, and they trusted that He had given it, even in the roll of the dice. There was no reason to doubt. I, too, began to trust that when I asked for guidance, God gave it. The end.

A greater test of my faith, however, came in trusting that even if the outcome of my decision didn't unfold as I hoped, it didn't mean it wasn't the God-guided choice. It just meant I couldn't see the whole picture, and God could. "Who is able to advise the Spirit of the Lord? Who knows enough to give him advice or teach him? Has the Lord ever needed anyone's advice? Does he need instruction about what is good? Did someone teach him what is right or show him the path of justice? No . . ." (Isaiah 40:13–15a NLT). Thank God we don't need to understand everything.

Father, Jesus, Holy Spirit, thank You for caring
enough to ensure Your will for me will be accomplished
in my life. Teach me Your ways. Amen.

Day 46

Joy From Within

NIKI

I'D DO ALMOST ANYTHING TO AVOID hard conversations. Having
to tell someone something they don't want to hear or will find hard
to accept fills me with anxiety and dread. Might our conversation
be the beginning of the end of our relationship? Sometimes though,
hard conversations are unavoidable if the relationship is one I cherish.
Paul had to have that kind of conversation through his letters with
the believers of the church at Corinth. It pained him (2 Corinthians
2:4), just as conflict pains me. But he loved them too much to allow
them to be misled by false teachers. Even in his own suffering, the
very thought of the believers there brought Paul comfort *and great
joy!* He loved them with an abiding love, and he had confidence in
them standing strong for the gospel truth no matter what lies some
were telling.

Is it possible to know joy when walking through a hard season?
It's not always easy, but it's possible. No matter my circumstances,
the one thing consistently stirring my heart to joy is knowing my
loved ones will spend eternity with Jesus. Everything of this life pales

in comparison to that knowledge. The "hard" of this life loses some of its edge when I remind myself this earth is not our home; we're only passing through. One day, we'll be forever in paradise with our Lord and Savior. The secret to joy is living in the now with our eyes on eternity—living with an eternal perspective, a Jesus-focused life.

Has anyone ever asked you who will be in heaven because of you? It's a thought-provoking, convicting, and important question. Jesus gave us a mission with the great commission, "Go therefore and make disciples of all nations" (Matthew 28:19). An abiding joy comes with knowing not only that you will be in heaven, but there will also be others there because of you. Let's never be afraid to tell someone about our Jesus. There is unmerited joy in salvation!

Paul was filled with joy when he thought about the believers in Corinth, even in the midst of affliction. He knew they would be with him in heaven one day. May we finish our race with the same confident joy.

Praise God! Joy Is a Gift!

CONSTANCE

HAVE YOU HAD A SEASON of exceeding joy in your life? As I write, I'm in a season of contentment and deep joy radiating in my soul. I'm surprised by the outflow of comfort and boldness created by this "seismic type" shift within me. My heart longed for the spirit of joy for months, but I had surrendered to a state of being numb to life, and then the shift occurred in my soul. Shouldn't this joy be the norm in our lives?

But what happens when an evil event occurs in our country or our lives? Suddenly, we're grappling with the intricacy of expressing and experiencing joy while in the midst of the grief we're feeling. How can we walk in joy and grief at the same time? Are we permitted to be joyful when evil is perpetrated on people?

The gifts of the Spirit are from God for us to enjoy and for the benefit of others. Joy is a gift! Praise God for it! Scripture reminds us to be joyful in whatever circumstance we find ourselves, to shout joyfully before our Lord, and to count it all joy when one enters into trials. But joy in grief?

C.S. Lewis, after much deliberation, concludes in his book, *Surprised by Joy*,[1] that joy is not an object or a fleeting emotion but a deeper way of being that's available to everyone. No matter what trial or circumstance we grieve, we still hold the inner joy, deep inside our soul, that comes from Jesus Christ to keep us steady.

The perplexities of life remind us to lean into the presence of God where fullness of joy is found. As Paul said, "In all our affliction, I am overflowing with joy." Remember, the joy of the Lord is our strength. One way to usher in joy is through gratefulness. I love this quote by Brother David Steindl-Rast, an Austrian American Benedictine monk, author, and lecturer, "It is not joy that makes us grateful; it is gratitude that makes us joyful."

Most of us understand happiness and joy when they are connected to events or possessions, but deep, abiding, immovable joy is very different. This joy is connected to God. It changes everything. He wants this kind of joy for you.

---

1   Lewis, C.S., *Surprised by Joy: The Shape of My Early Life,* HarperOne; Reissue Edition, February 14, 2017.

Loving Father, thank You for the privilege of joy that comes from our salvation in Christ. Help me, Lord, to shout from the mountaintops the joy of knowing Jesus! Amen.

Day 47

Then our mouth was filled with laughter, and our tongue
with shouts of joy; then they said among the nations,
"The Lord has done great things for them."
—Psalm 126:2

Find the Laughter in Your Soul. It's There!

CONSTANCE

I CAN ONLY IMAGINE THE EFFERVESCENT joy our Lord receives from our laughter! After all, a merry heart is good for one's health. I would argue it's a quicker remedy, at times, than some medicine. Laughter is one of the best forms of therapy for those of us who have dealt with depression at points in our lives. The power of laughter, especially those belly laughs, can trigger great joy in our hearts and move us from self-obsession to a healthier place.

Have you experienced the emotional shift that occurs when spontaneous laughter erupts between you and friends? So much joy floods the atmosphere, and your cares are whisked away, at least for a time. Even a funny movie can do wonders and remove the hanging cloud over our heads. Laughter lightens our hearts and offers healing for our dysregulated emotions. Our bodies need a release of the stress and tension. Laughter, oftentimes, is the perfect solution; at least it was for Niki and me!

On a mission trip to Africa in 2018, we experienced the power of laughter. The week was exhaustingly difficult, mostly physically but also emotionally. Of course, we were excited for the opportunity to help the medical team provide assistance to disenfranchised Togolese families living in grass/mud huts. They wore beautiful smiles and colorful attire. They owned barely anything but always displayed love and appreciation for us. It humbled us and gave us inner joy.

Niki and I would return to our room after dinner each evening to prep for the next day. After a cold shower, it would happen. We would laugh about everything—the wonky things about our room, the outrageous occurrences of the day, anything and everything, even ourselves. I'm talking about belly laughter with tears streaming down our faces. Laughter got us through the ten days. God knew exactly what was necessary for His girls.

Even years later, recalling our trip, or any experiences shared together, we easily find ourselves in belly laughter all over again. It's so interesting how laughter repeats itself in the stories we share. They're just as funny every time we think of them.

I'll leave you with words from Martin Luther King, Jr., "It is cheerful to God when you rejoice or laugh from the bottom of your heart." Good advice!

A Belly Laugh Is Good for the Spirit

NIKI

IN 2018, CONSTANCE AND I FOUND ourselves in Africa on a medical mission trip with our church. Neither one of us has a medical background, but there were many nonmedical roles to fill. Having never served in this way before, we didn't quite know what to expect.

We knew seeing people in pain would be hard, but what was most unexpected were the times of our uncontrolled laughter!

We shared a room and a double bed. The bathroom had no hot water, and the toilet couldn't even handle toilet paper. We felt fortunate to have an air conditioner stuck in the wall above the window, as it was summer and hot. We felt less fortunate when that air conditioner turned out to sound like a jet engine on takeoff. We'd get up in the morning, look at each other, and burst out laughing over the ear-splitting noise. It was only because we were bone-weary tired that we were able to sleep at all. Our room with the built-in jet engine was just one of many things over that ten-day trip that made us laugh. Even now, years later, when we talk about that trip, we wind up belly laughing 'til our sides ache!

Laughter is so good for both the body and the spirit. And it's also good for the world to see Christ followers live with joy and laughter. It's contagious, and our joy could be what draws others to want to know Jesus. We've been given the greatest gift in Jesus, and yet so often, we walk around as though the weight of the world is on our shoulders. Life can be hard. Believe me, I know that truth as well as anyone. But no matter our circumstances, no one (not even Satan and his evil tactics) can separate us from the love of God in Christ Jesus. There's no greater reason for joy and laughter!

God tells us to always be joyful, to never stop praying, and to be thankful no matter what (1 Thessalonians 5:16–18). These are three instructions we're all capable of when we keep our eyes fixed on Jesus and are mindful of the gift He's already given us. May we be joyful, prayerful, and so grateful that the world's curiosity is stirred to wanting what we have. Don't let anyone steal your joy. Laugh with abandon! It's good for the soul. Having Jesus and having joy go hand in hand.

Father, Son, and Holy Spirit, thank You for loving me unfailingly. Help me show the world Your love through a joyful spirit and even laughter. Amen.

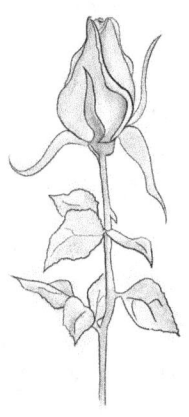

Day 48

And the peace of God, which surpasses all understanding,
will guard your hearts and your minds in Christ Jesus.

—*Philippians 4:7*

Take It to the Lord in Prayer

NIKI

HAVE YOU EVER WRESTLED with a decision, praying that if you made the right one, God would fill you with peace? I remember in the 1980s, Yuma, Arizona was a Marine Corps duty station option for us. It was a wonderful job opportunity for Joe, but neither of us really wanted to spend three years in the desert. Ultimately, we let a fortune cookie at the end of a meal decide for us. The cookie's fortune said, "You will take a trip to the desert." Boy, did I second-guess that one! But lately, I've been learning not to second-guess my decisions. If I've given it to God, I can trust His guidance, direction, and peace will come. Big and small, God cares about every decision we make.

Paul writes this verse immediately after instruction to take everything to God in prayer. This "peace *of* God" is different than the "peace *with* God" we experience when we surrender our lives to Jesus. That "with God" kind of peace is reconciliation into relationship with Him. The "of God" peace Paul writes about is a blessing God gives us in exchange for giving Him our cares and worries.

God never wants us to carry any burden on our own. It's what Jesus meant when He said, "Take my yoke upon you . . . and you will find rest for your souls. For my yoke is easy and my burden is light" (Matthew 11:29–30). A yoke is a piece of farm equipment that binds two animals together to share the load of pulling a wagon or other piece of equipment. Jesus desires to help us carry the burdens that cause us worry. He shoulders what we don't have the strength to shoulder on our own.

Worry originates in the mind (anxiety-producing thoughts) and festers in the heart (spiraling feelings). May our first anxious thoughts bring us to our knees before the Lord. What a privilege we have, through the death and resurrection of Jesus, to come into the throne room of God. God's mercy, grace, help, and presence all comprise His blessing of peace. Prayer conquers worry and guards our hearts and minds with God's gift of peace. Pray without ceasing, about all things great and small, and receive the gift of God that defies understanding. Yoke yourself to Jesus and rest in Him, sweet friends.

Peace Like a Flowing River

CONSTANCE

CAN WE TRULY EXPERIENCE PEACE? Is there an underlying unease prohibiting us from fully living a peaceful life, regardless of what is going on in the world?

Although I enjoy having friends over for dinner, I still experience some disquiet in the days leading up to their arrival. I try to dispel those unwelcome feelings by focusing on other things, such as switching pictures on my walls and moving knick-knacks around, anything but the dinner. When my friends arrive, I'm relaxed and ready for a wonderful time.

Once, a friend invited a group to her house to show us how to host an easy party. She provided her lovely home, gorgeous backyard, and beverages. Each guest brought her favorite appetizer. Twenty ladies arrived with a variety of food and hearts full of excitement. Margaret showed us how a gathering of people who desire to be together can be simple. No one was overloaded with responsibility, and participation created peace not anxiety. It was beautiful.

Jesus encouraged us not to be afraid or allow our hearts to be troubled. Paul, who was familiar with suffering, advised us to let the peace of Christ rule in our hearts always. Peace is one of the fruits of the Spirit available to believers in Christ. A Google search shows about four hundred references to peace in the Bible, depending on which translation you're using. So why are we not walking in peace?

I believe, at least for myself, it's a flesh problem—my passions and desires drive me to seek perfection. In those moments, I'm submitting to the flesh instead of yielding to the Spirit. My spirit, and maybe yours, wants to live in peace, to walk in kingdom authority over anxiety, fear, and self-absorption. The calm and beautiful life God wants for His children comes from the Spirit.

Begin today. Let's ask for peace, receive it, and enjoy our friends and family. We can live freely in peace, even when sometimes experiencing anxiety, for God is our strength and our shield.

Father, I long for the peace that surpasses understanding. Help me to guard my heart and mind in Christ. I desire peace in all things. I reject anxiety and fear. Amen.

Day 49

> *Moreover, he said to me, "Son of man, all my words that I shall speak to you receive in your heart, and hear with your ears."*
>
> —*Ezekiel 3:10*

Oh No. Not That, God!

CONSTANCE

THERE'S A BEAUTIFUL TREE-LINED lake full of wildlife in my dog-friendly community. Each day, I find great pleasure prayer-walking around the lake for a time of quiet reflection. But, recently, I noticed large piles of dog poop in the lovely grassy areas. I was extremely agitated by the lack of concern exhibited by certain pet owners. Bags are generously provided, as well as disposal boxes to make this task convenient.

As I walked, I began grumbling to God about the situation. But soon, God interrupted my rant, *Well, Constance, you could pick it up!* I hadn't considered picking it up myself. Why would I lower myself to clean up someone else's dog's mess? I didn't want to do it, period. "Are you serious, God?" He was.

My attitude was horrible; I was complaining and definitely not praying. I wanted the dog owners to clean up after their pets! So when God spoke to me, I listened, even though I didn't want to act. I eventually assumed the responsibility of the "Poop Fairy," scooping up the "deposits" left by those precious pets, then ferrying the green doggie bags into the disposal containers. It was humbling!

It didn't take long for me to discover that through that small thing, God wanted to show me something. Instead of complaining, assume responsibility. If it bothered me that much, I could fix it. Within a few days, my bad attitude turned into gratitude. God was personally concerned about me, just as He is about you. It's important to hear when He speaks and to respond.

My job is over for the time being. Pet owners seem more aware of their responsibilities, and I'm not inclined to do it so much. My heart is lighter, though, because God softened the hard edges of my attitude.

Listen With Your Heart

NIKI

IT'S BEEN SAID THAT THE longest journey you will ever take is the eighteen inches from your head to your heart. In today's verse, the Lord was cautioning Ezekiel against such a tragedy, and He means to caution us, too.

God gave us the truth in His Word. It's near to us; we're able to hold it in our very hands. Yet, what He wants is that we hold it in our hearts. God gives us His Word to change us, and change always begins in the heart. However, we can hear His Word with our ears and never receive it in our hearts.

Jesus explained, "The good person out of the good treasure of his heart produces good, and the evil person out of his evil treasure produces evil, for out of the abundance of the heart his mouth speaks" (Luke 6:45). When the Holy Spirit changes our hearts through God's Word, we're drawn closer to Him. God made us for relationship with Him, now and for all of eternity. It took me decades to understand that truth. I knew God in my head, but I didn't let His truth

170

penetrate the depths of my heart. Yet, God pursued me—for a very long time—until the Spirit reached my heart. Suddenly, Scripture came alive for me. My relationship with the Lord became my most cherished relationship. Thank God! Thank God He doesn't leave us to only know Him intellectually, but He pursues a heart-to-heart relationship with us.

Let us open not only our ears to His Word, but let us also listen and receive with our hearts. A deep relationship with our Lord and Savior changes us from the inside out.

Father God, I desire to hear Your voice. Thank You for not giving up in Your pursuit of me. Help me to invite You into the depths of my heart. Amen.

Day 50

And James and John, the sons of Zebedee, came up to him and said to him, "Teacher, we want you to do for us whatever we ask of you." And he said to them, "What do you want me to do for you?" And they said to him, "Grant us to sit, one at your right hand and one at your left, in your glory."

—Mark 10:35–37

Me First, Lord!

NIKI

THE FACT THIS CONVERSATION TOOK place astonishes me! James and John were among the first disciples Jesus called to follow Him. They left their nets and their father at once and went with Jesus. Yet, in this conversation we can see the universal human condition—pride. In Matthew's account of the same story (Matthew 20:20–21), it's James and John's mother who first approaches Jesus with this request on behalf of her sons. Her request may have been born of the pride in her own heart.

When I was in second grade, my mother intervened on my behalf, too. My school put on an annual play. Each grade did their own musical production. I don't remember what ours was, but there was a scene at the end where several little girls were escorted across the stage by little boys while someone sang, "There She Is, Miss America." I was not chosen to be one of the Miss Americas. It could be because I had a severe overbite and short hair permed into a mass of frizz.

Beauty did not come to mind when you saw me! But I had been the flower girl in my sister's wedding the previous year, and so, I had a sweet gown. Because of the gown, my mother intervened and asked I be made a Miss America. The next thing I knew, there I was, Miss America, feeling embarrassed as I walked across the stage in my baby blue chiffon and puff of frizz. I knew it was only because my mother insisted.

Pride is at the heart of most, if not all, sins. It's hard to name a sin that doesn't have something to do with pride. "Self first" is at the core of every one of us. Pride, like other heart issues, is something we're helpless to change on our own. It's only through the transforming work of the Holy Spirit that we can tame our self-first attitude and truly love like Jesus does—sacrificially. No one who puts self first gives his life for another.

Our goal in this earthly life is to become more like Jesus. God uses all kinds of circumstances in the life of a surrendered heart to do just that. As a second grader, I didn't understand my mother's heart in intervening about my part in the play. I realize now that pride can sometimes be couched as love, as I believe it might have been for her. I wonder if James and John thought the same about their mother's request.

God's work in us is ongoing, and only He knows what we need to experience to fully become the people He created us to be. Give Him your heart and trust Him to do what only He can do.

Questions and Requests

CONSTANCE

AS A CHILD, MY FAMILY didn't celebrate birthdays or Christmas.

Gifts were randomly given throughout the year. I asked for nothing but hoped for something. Now, friends sometimes ask me, "What can we do for you?" I can be timid in saying what I need or want. I was raised to be independent. I couldn't depend on anyone to do what they said they would do. However, over many years, I've watched the way others have accepted *my* offer of assistance, and slowly, I began to accept graciously their desire to lend a hand, have lunch out, bring a gift, or whatever it is, saying thank you. I witnessed the joy in giving and receiving.

My ability to ask for help and receive gifts from others grew. It takes humility to ask, and humility is a beautiful attribute of Christ-followers. I remind myself, and you can too, that God inspires people to bless us. We can do both! Help others and receive help ourselves.

It seems James and John were comfortable approaching Jesus with their request for Him to do whatever they asked of Him. But their appeal seems forward, a demand of sorts. Jesus responded as He usually did to those He helped, softly and incisively, asking, "What do you want me to do for you?" James and John desired what appeared to be positions of authority when they requested to be seated at Jesus' right and left hands in glory. They presumed Jesus' kingdom would be earthly and free them from the Roman rule under which they lived.

The brothers clearly didn't know what they were asking. Would they be willing to submit to the suffering of Christ to get to glory? Probably not. Jesus told them He didn't yet have the power to grant them their request. His authority came from God, and He did only what the Father instructed Him to do. The sons of Zebedee could have benefited from some discernment about asking for the right things. I would have benefitted from the same in several situations myself.

Interestingly, the *risen* Jesus later appeared to the disciples announcing all authority had been given to Him. Jesus then handed the authority to us to carry on His mission (Matthew 28:18–20). How well are we stewarding that authority?

Lord, continue Your work in me. Take out my selfish heart and give me a tender, responsive, and humble heart. Enable me to release control and embrace the authority You have given me. Amen.

Day 51

Jesus said to him, "The one who has bathed does not
need to wash, except for his feet, but is completely clean.
And you are clean, but not every one of you."

—John 13:10

Humility and Clean Feet

CONSTANCE

I HAD THE PLEASURE AND OPPORTUNITY to live in Hawaii for ten years. The custom of leaving one's shoes, usually flip-flops, outside the door when entering a home was a new practice for me. I loved this custom, but I was unsuccessful keeping up the practice when I returned to the mainland. In Hawaiian culture, taking off your shoes is meant not only for cleanliness but also as an expression of hospitality, friendship, and respect from those traveling and stopping at your home.

In ancient times, foot washing was a religious ritual for cleanliness in holy places and is still often practiced today. During the Feast of Passover, when Jesus prepared to wash the feet of his disciples, Peter wasn't having it. Jesus told Peter if He didn't wash his feet, Peter wouldn't belong to Him. Peter agreed, and Jesus washed not only Peter's feet but the feet of all the disciples.

Jesus went on to explain to Peter that he was clean, but not all of them were. Could it be the disciples were clean because they had given their hearts to Jesus and were baptized (bathed) into a new life? It was also the words Jesus spoke to them that made them clean (John

15:3). Judas, however, took Satan's bait and was about to betray Jesus. He was the one who was unclean.

When I came to Jesus with an open heart, in need of forgiveness and seeking restoration, I needed a foot washing. There will be times when I'm on the receiving end and others when I'm the one offering, like the woman who came to wash Jesus' feet. She entered the room where Jesus was reclining, washed his feet with her tears, wiped them with her hair, and then poured expensive ointment over his feet. This woman was desperate; she needed forgiveness, and she humbled herself before Jesus. He lovingly gave her everything she needed.

How about you? Do you need a foot washing today?

God Knows Our Hearts and Our Feet!

NIKI

ANOTHER LIFETIME AGO, right out of high school, I became a hairstylist. In those days, hairstylists also did manicures and, ugh, pedicures. So I know a little something about the repugnance of feet! In Christ's day, the lowliest of servants would get the feet assignment, and yet, Jesus served his beloved disciples in this lowliest of ways by washing all of their feet. Christ's humble action stirred up Peter's pride as he objected to Jesus washing his feet.

The most obvious lesson here for us is in the posture of our hearts. A servant's heart begins in a place of humility. Christ's humble service came out of love. The same truth applies to us. I once heard a Christian counselor say, "Every relationship you're in is for the good of the other person." Jesus modeled the truth of that statement perfectly in action and word.

The second lesson is crucial. Jesus said, "The one who has bathed does not need to wash, except for his feet . . . ." The critical difference here is between bathed and washed. Once we are bathed by Jesus' blood, we are forever clean and no longer have a need to be bathed again by Christ's blood. Our salvation through Christ's death and resurrection is assured once and forever. But why then the need to repeatedly wash the feet?

Sinners saved through Jesus' death and resurrection are still sinners. We walk in a sinful, cursed, and broken world. So while our salvation is assured, our need for forgiveness is ongoing. That is the need of the daily washing of our feet. While the Holy Spirit strengthens us to stand against temptation, we can't do it perfectly. God doesn't expect us to. He knows how weak we are. God provides the way for us to be reconciled with Him, no matter the failure. In 1 John 1:9, He promises, "If we confess our sins, he is faithful and just to forgive us our sins and to cleanse us from all unrighteousness." Bathed forevermore and washed continually.

Lord, make me an instrument of Your love,
Your service, for all people. Amen.

Day 52

By day the Lord commands his steadfast love, and at night his song is with me, a prayer to the God of my life.

—Psalm 42:8

Sing It Out!

NIKI

HAVE YOU EVER AWAKENED in the middle of the night with a praise and worship song running through your head? Or upon waking first thing in the morning, a worship song is on your lips? I have, many times, and I love when it happens. It brings my first thoughts to the Lord, and it makes me think I was, perhaps, dreaming of God when I awoke.

Psalm 42 is a lament. The writer is going through a difficult season, and he wonders why he doesn't feel close to God. He laments not being in Jerusalem to worship. But then in verse 8, he reminds himself of who God is and how He loves him. He reminds himself that he can worship anywhere. I need to remind myself of those facts often. Life can be hard sometimes, and we find ourselves wondering where God is in our suffering.

It's funny how things can tend to feel less threatening during the day. It feels easier to remember God is with us and He loves us, no matter what, in the daylight. The author of Psalm 42 seems to recognize it, too. The dark can tend to feel more threatening. His response during the night is to draw close to the Lord through songs of worship. Songs are his prayer. They often are for me, too.

Truth be told, I most often wake up with worship songs running through my mind and on my lips when I've spent time during the previous day singing praises to my King. When I walk the dog, I listen to praise and worship music, and I sing it out in my full voice. I've been singing as I walk for several years. So far, no one has told me to shut up. It has become to me a "mini-ministry." I like to think that whatever I'm singing when I pass someone is just what they need to hear to draw them to Jesus. I don't know if that's true or not, but God can do all things.

Love Explodes at Starbucks

CONSTANCE

I'M A CURIOUS PERSON, ANTICIPATING times God will reveal His love to me, but on one particular day, I didn't expect His love to overwhelm me, especially while getting a coffee at Starbucks. A surge of enormous love suddenly filled my entire being, and it wasn't just my love of coffee! I was overwhelmed by love and immense joy. It was so strong, I thought I would burst. I loved everyone in Starbucks that day through the joy overflowing from my heart, the huge smile on my face, conversations with those I encountered, and a willingness to be kind in a not so kind world. My capacity to contain this surge of love was limited, so I asked God to pull back just a bit. Was I experiencing the fullness of God in my life that day? I don't know, but I found God's love overpowering, expansive, beautiful, and wild. In hindsight, I wish I hadn't asked him to pull back. Today, I would go with His flow and see where it led.

Some definitions of love characterize it as a strong affection, devotedness, passion, tenderness for another person, something one cherishes. Love encompasses feelings and emotions through various types—Philia, love between friends and family; Eros, love between a husband and wife; Agape, love between God and His children. Many of us have experienced Christ's love in exceptional ways. We certainly know it when it happens!

As Christ followers, we know God is love. We also know Jesus' love for the world through His sacrifice for us. Paul writes in Romans 8:38–39, that nothing can separate us from God's love. His love can't be measured, but we can grow in comprehension of the breadth, length, height, and depth of it.

Developing a love relationship involves trust. Can we trust those to whom we give our love? Can we trust God's love? We're flawed children of the God of mercy all walking our way home. I still struggle with loving and feeling loved, but God and I are working on it. There's so much more of God's infinite love available for us, my friends. Love changes everything! How are you receiving love and giving love to others?

Father God, Lord Jesus, Holy Spirit, thank You for Your steadfast love for me every moment of every day. Put Your song in my heart. Amen.

Day 53

Do not be conformed to this world, but be transformed by the renewal of your mind that by testing you may discern what is the will of God, what is good and acceptable and perfect.

—*Romans 12:2*

Dexter, Us, Jesus

CONSTANCE

WATCHING A KITTEN TRY TO pull a stone out of a large bowl was intriguing to me but extremely frustrating for the kitten. With one paw in the bowl, Dexter worked for several long minutes, trying to pull the stone up the glass only to watch it drop back down. Though he worked hard and was patient, eventually he accepted defeat and went on to something else. That rock wasn't coming out of the bowl that day.

As it was with Dexter, so it is with us, pushing and pulling, striving and digging. Each day, we have agendas full of endless responsibilities and cravings that need satisfying. Firmly established in culture, we join the race to achieve, only slowly realizing something isn't working. Our children are glued to screens, dinners are fast food, and time off is relegated to a one-week vacation a year. That kind of lifestyle doesn't give us the nourishment we need. At the end of the day, exhausted, we surrender to our pillows, unable to fall asleep because our minds can't rest. Most days our to-do lists carry over to the next squirrelly day. And on it goes!

Listening to our bodies, we sense fatigue. Our souls yearn for calm and peace, and our minds are so fragmented we can't figure out why we're disjointed in our thinking and prone to a critical mindset. We're desperately looking for what we need, yet we don't know what we're looking for.

Jesus lived simply and with intention. He had a full plate of ministry, miracles, and facing criticism. Yet, Jesus seemed to do it all seamlessly. He made intimate times alone with His Father a priority, so that he could accomplish the work He came to do. In His humanness, He felt the emotions we feel. Why wouldn't He? How else could He understand our struggles and pain? We worship Him as the Son of God, but He also was the Son of Man.

Conformity to this world will not bring solitude and peace or closeness to the Father. But, renewing our minds with the Word, sitting in His presence, and discerning the good and perfect things we should consider for our lives will bring true nourishment. Don't hurry, friends. Breathe deeply, let go of the worthless, and let God give you life.

What Is Good and Acceptable and Perfect?

NIKI

IN 2020, I DECIDED TO change my two-glass-per-night wine habit. I had been wrestling with the Holy Spirit over it for a couple years. I rationalized I was never intoxicated, nor did I think I was dependent on wine. But I was tired of the internal battle, knowing God was calling me to change this habit and resisting Him every step of the way. When I finally surrendered to what I knew God wanted of me,

I looked for resources to help. I found Rachel Hart's *Take a Break From Drinking* podcast. There are more than one hundred seventy-five episodes, and I listened to most of them.

Rachel's podcast introduced me to the "think, feel, act cycle." The concept demonstrates how our actions come from our feelings/emotions, which originate with a thought. The think, feel, act cycle has been studied and proven. It's possible to work backward from an action (having a glass of wine) to identify the feeling that spurred it (maybe anxiety), all the way back to the thought where the feeling originated (Why is my life so stressful?).

So, if our desire is not to conform to the world and to be transformed, it all begins with our thoughts. But how do we change our thoughts? Have you ever tried not to think about something? When you're trying not to think about it, what are you doing? You're thinking about it!

The New Living Translation of Romans 12:2 says, ". . . let God transform you into a new person by changing the way you think." God takes on the responsibility of transforming (or sanctifying) us by working in our thought process. I've discovered the easiest and best way for me to cooperate with the Holy Spirit to renew my mind and change my thoughts is to replace a negative or world-conforming thought with a thought focused on the Lord and eternity. It's what living with an eternal perspective is all about. It takes practice, but as Christ followers, we have the power of the Holy Spirit to help us. The Holy Spirit is able to lead our thoughts to what is good, acceptable, perfect, and worthy of praise. Who is *all* of these things? Jesus.

Holy Spirit, I surrender all to You. Lead my
thoughts always to Jesus. Amen.

Day 54

*"Be still, and know that I am God. I will be exalted
among the nations, I will be exalted in the earth."*

—*Psalm 46:10*

How Can I Know Him?

NIKI

BEING STILL AND QUIET with the Lord is essential to hearing His
voice. But this verse talks not about hearing God but of knowing God.
What part do *we* play in God revealing Himself and His character to
us? And what is the result of our coming to know Him in a deeply
intimate way?

The Hebrew word translated here as "be still" is *rapha*, which means
"to be weak, to let go, to release." In other words, coming to know
God isn't so much about quieting our minds as it is about letting go of
control—surrendering ourselves fully to the Lord's control. Oftentimes,
it's in seasons of hard, dark trial where we recognize we don't have
control over just about anything. Coming to that realization allows
us to cling to Jesus instead of to our illusion of control. It's where we
come to know God in ways we wouldn't otherwise know Him. And
this knowledge is why it's possible to be thankful even in suffering.

Surrender has such a negative connotation in our culture. It suggests
weakness. But as God so often does, He turns our cultural meaning
on its head, for surrender ultimately brings us into glorious freedom!
Over the years, I've learned so much about surrender and unexpected

freedom. My greatest lesson came in taking all of the shame, hurt, and sorrow from my childhood that I carried for decades and laying it on Jesus' shoulders.

God never intended for me to carry those heavy burdens myself, but for the longest time, I didn't understand. I thought burying those feelings and denying the truth of my story was the way to freedom. The only thing those methods did was intensify my shame. Only in speaking the truth of my story and crying out my feelings of shame to the Lord did I see how His Light was beginning to change everything I believed about myself. Surrender brought release from shame. Just the way God intended. How sweet is the love and care of our Lord!

In releasing our illusion of control into God's hands, the world's eyes might be opened to see His power, His grace, His mercy, His majesty. Someone is always watching. One day, all will exalt the Lord. May we trust Him enough now to surrender all.

Knowing God in Stillness

CONSTANCE

WHILE IN TURKEY ON HOLIDAY, I visited the historic Blue Mosque in Istanbul. I had the unique opportunity to be in the mosque before they closed the doors to non-Muslims for the "call to prayer." Five times a day, Muslims stop all activity for prayer. As I watched from a distance, I was inspired by their commitment, dedication, and unified prayer times. Could I incorporate a similar rhythm of specific times each day to create space, five or even twenty minutes, in silence for reflection and prayer?

We need solitude appointments of stillness in our day for our spirits, souls, and bodies. Our yearning hearts long to hear the sweet whisper of His voice and experience the comfort of His closeness. "Be still, and know that I am God" is the call of the Spirit. God rested from creating on the seventh day. Slowing down our pace is life extending. Practicing sabbath may begin with worship and fellowship at church, but it can also include family time, a walk in nature, reading a book, a nap, or a special meal. Being with the Lord, resting our bodies, and bringing refreshment to our minds is the purpose.

God is inviting us into the beautiful discipline of stillness—a practice of creating space and time to be with Him, to clear the constant distraction of the mind, and to rest. It's here we enter a place of knowing.

Is there a special chair or room, a garden, the porch swing, or even your parked car under a tree where you can be still and abide? Explore with five to ten minutes in the morning, sitting quietly in prayer. Clear your mind, be still, and be with your Father. "Listen to me in silence" (Isaiah 41:1).

The exalted God of the earth wants us to know Him! Stillness creates deeper intimacy with God. Jesus found time to be alone, to hear His Father's words, and then to give them to His followers. If Jesus needed time alone, then so do we.

"... in quietness and trust shall be your strength" (Isaiah 30:15).

Father, teach me to know You through times of solitude and stillness. Help me surrender all control to You and trust in Your plan for me. Through my surrender, Lord, may I know You as deeply as I possibly can. Amen.

Day 55

"Whoever loves his life loses it, and whoever hates his life in this world will keep it for eternal life."

—*John 12:25*

The Good Ole Life

CONSTANCE

AFTER TWO YEARS OF THE PANDEMIC, all I wanted was to have my good life back. Everything had changed. Fear consumed and disrupted our ability to think logically, businesses closed, many lost jobs, others worked from home, and the housing market exploded. In the midst of it all, I made decisions that flip-flopped my life. I wanted the life I had, the home I sold in 2021, and things to return to normal.

Remember Lot's wife (Genesis 19:26)? Angels led Lot and his family out of Sodom, a corrupt and immoral city. They were instructed to leave and not look back. But Lot's wife turned, and she became a pillar of salt. What would make her disregard the angels' warning? I imagine she wanted one more look at the city she loved, perhaps longing for the life she had there, the routine, her home, and familiar friends. What heartbreak to have wanted something so badly that even angels weren't able to persuade her to let go and look forward to a "life-giving" future.

God created this earth to be enjoyed. Traveling sparks inspiration and wonder for me and gratitude for His creation. The loving community I experience when sharing meals and events with friends and family while enjoying the fruits of the earth's bounty are blessings to enjoy. It feels like the "good life." Jesus' words challenge me when He reminds me to hate my life in this world to keep it, and they should. But I'm not always eager to let go of the desires that make my life comfortable.

John 12:25 gives a clear understanding of what Jesus desires for us. It's not so much that we love our lives; it's whether that love is greater than the love we have for Him. Will we be like Lot's wife, longing for the familiar, or will we long for the Life Giver?

We may love God, but are our hearts divided between the "good ole life" promised by the world and the "eternal life" promised by Jesus? When we turn everything and everyone over to Him, He gives us His everything. When we sit with the discomfort of Jesus' words, we ultimately come to understand the deeper truth of surrendering to Christ in order to find our truest selves.

Me, Myself, and I

NIKI

SOMETIMES, BEING HONEST WITH YOURSELF is the hardest truth of all. I confess I still sometimes struggle with idols. They're just not made of silver or gold. They're made of self and of control. Self shows her power over me most often when my comfort is threatened. Control rears her head when plans go awry or interruptions are unremitting.

My idols, like most in these times, are all about me and my life. They keep my focus on me. But if my focus is on me, my life loses its value in making a lasting difference in the lives of others. With myself as idol, I waste my life. I miss the mission and purpose God has for me, and that is the loss that comes with loving my life over the welfare and well-being of those around me. Chasing after the things of this world, pleasure and comfort included, leads to a wasted life in view of eternity.

In the second half of John 12:25, Jesus describes a fruitful life. It's the life Jesus Himself lived. He was humble of heart, always taking the time to let others interrupt Him. He lived His life, even to the point of death, to fulfill God's mission and purpose for Him. For us, to lay down our lives in this world is to give up our illusion of control and to surrender to the Lord's control. We give our lives to Jesus, and He gives us everything that truly matters—forgiveness, unfailing love, grace, and mercy in this life and an endless eternity with Him in paradise.

Paul, too, understood the importance of valuing Jesus over his own life. "Indeed, I count everything as loss because of the surpassing worth of knowing Christ Jesus my Lord. For his sake I have suffered the loss of all things and count them as rubbish, in order that I may gain Christ" (Philippians 3:8). May we do the same. Jesus is the One who changes everything for us and about us. He gives priceless value to our lives. Without Him, we're lost, and sorrowfully, our lives are wasted.

Father, thank You for digging deeper into my heart to show me where my desires lie. Help me to follow Your example and to live my life fully surrendered to Your plan, will, and purpose. Amen.

Day 56

*The Lord said to Abraham, "Why did Sarah laugh and say,
'Shall I indeed bear a child now that I am old?' Is anything
too hard for the Lord? At the appointed time I will return
to you, about this time next year, and Sarah shall have
a son." But Sarah denied it saying, "I did not laugh," for
she was afraid. He said, "No, but you did laugh."*

—Genesis 18:13–15

I'll Deny It . . .

NIKI

I CAN RELATE TO SARAH in these verses—not pregnancy in old age, thank the Lord, but to the thought likely going through her mind as she laughed. *I'll believe it when I see it!* Most of us have probably said or thought those words at one time. Needing to see something to believe it, though, is the opposite of faith. Faith tells us to believe, so we can see!

Fear caused Sarah to deny what she had done. Isn't it like that with just about every lie we tell? We're afraid of something or someone when lies come from our lips. But denial sometimes goes deeper than fear. For decades, I denied the effect that childhood sexual abuse had on my adult life. When I was finally able to share my story and begin the long process of healing, I learned that denial can also be a lack of faith. I wasn't able to trust the reality of what God had allowed and still believe He is good. So, in denial, I created an alternate

191

reality—the abuse was not a big deal. It was years ago, so I needed to forget about it; it had no effect on my life now. My denial was just as much a lie as Sarah's.

Sarah did have a son like the Lord had promised. I love that her failures didn't keep God from moving in her life. God redeemed her story with a promise fulfilled. God has redeemed my story, too. I've shared my story countless times over the fifteen years since God called me to begin healing. It's true what's been said: the area of deepest pain in your life will likely be your greatest testimony and ministry opportunity. God never wastes anything. Even pain has purpose. My pain brought me to serving in a ministry that helps women survivors of childhood sexual abuse find healing in their stories, freedom from shame, and abundant life in Jesus.

Jesus said, ". . . and you will know the truth and the truth will set you free" (John 8:32). I believe it, *and* I've also seen it.

Laughter Into Blessing

CONSTANCE

FOR SIX YEARS, I PRAYED FOR A MIRACLE for my stepdaughter, Stephanie, and her husband. The years of waiting were like a roller coaster ride, with deep plunges, up, down, and around. The ride included encouragement but also times of disappointment. Sometimes, I wanted to give up.

Stephanie had endured a multitude of various medical procedures and surgery, acupuncture, and Chinese herbs, all to encourage a full-term pregnancy. Everything failed, including adoption. After years of emotional turbulence, physical pain, and expense, they made the decision to take a break from it all. Not long after, the news came that Stephanie was pregnant. She carried the baby to term, and the long-awaited miracle arrived! A beautiful baby girl named Gia was born, God's gift to us all. Oh what joy we experienced that day. Nothing is impossible for God!

Perhaps Sarah felt the way Stephanie did while waiting for a child, wanting to give up, thinking it was too late. So, when Sarah overheard the conversation between the Lord and Abraham regarding a child, she laughed. *I'm old, worn out, and my husband is even older,* she thought. But, when the Lord heard her laughter, He questioned Abraham, who had laughed himself when God told him he would have a child. Sarah, however, denied laughing. Maybe she didn't want to appear to doubt the Lord. Or perhaps the thought of being pregnant at ninety, with a one-hundred-year-old husband, was overwhelming and confusing. Imagine waiting seventy years and then being told you would have a son. I would probably laugh, too. God, the Creator of all things, was promising a miracle.

The season of longing for what we had hoped with Stephanie and her husband was full of sorrow and grief at times but also patience and, finally, answered prayer. When the miracle came, we were humbled and fell to our knees in worship and praise, gratitude, and repentance for any lack of trust.

Begin today, believe the unbelievable, allow your faith to flourish, and trust God, who is more engaged in your story than you could possibly know.

My Father, Your questions prompt me to seek better answers, more faith, greater trust. Help my unbelief when doubt slips in. Thank You, Jesus, for Your saving grace and undeserved mercy. Amen.

Day 57

But one thing I do: forgetting what lies behind and straining
forward to what lies ahead, I press on toward the goal for
the prize of the upward call of God in Christ Jesus.
—*Philippians 3:13b–14*

Pick Up That Anchor and Set Sail

CONSTANCE

SEBASTIAN WAS ELEVEN WHEN HIS DAD passed away from a violent assault. It was horrific. Sebastian didn't want to talk about his father's death because it made him sad. I took my pain to God on daily prayer walks. Even though Woody and I were divorced, every morning, I would get lost in the "what ifs." What if we had tried harder to make our marriage work? What if I had been more forgiving? What if . . . What if . . . What if . . . , and so it went each day for six months, and then, it happened.

One morning, the Lord spoke clearly to me, not audibly, but Spirit to spirit. It got my attention. I realized it was time to stop looking back and begin pressing forward. It was time to stop mulling over the grief, which always led me to greater sadness. I heard God speak to my heart and responded. I turned from regret and hopelessness to freedom to move forward with hope—we would be fine. Within days, I came across this Philippians verse confirming what I had heard from God, and I knew He was guiding me to new things. I was not denying the things behind that were painful and difficult, but pushing ahead through the discomfort and sadness. What was ahead for us was something so much greater, a prize of great price, everlasting life with Jesus.

Sometime later, I was drawn to Isaiah 43:18–19, "Behold, I am doing a new thing; now it springs forth, do you not perceive it? I will make a way in the wilderness and rivers in the desert." Is this not the most encouraging Scripture when going through a difficult season? "Rivers in the desert!" These verses were additional confirmation that God was doing a new thing in my son's life and mine.

God knows our pain, and He desires for us to press in to Him, pouring out our heartbreak. Then, He speaks through Scripture and whispers as we pray, bringing comfort to our souls.

God is always doing a new thing. He is making a way through the storm. All things are changing. Do we not perceive it? Are we buried in the past, the mistakes of a younger age? Perhaps it's time to lay those things down and press forward into what lies ahead, the upward call of God in Christ Jesus—eternal life.

Too Excited to Sleep!

NIKI

HAVE YOU EVER BEEN SO FILLED with anticipation you couldn't sleep? I grew up an hour from the Jersey shore. As a child, my family would take day trips to Seaside Heights. To my little girl eyes, Seaside was the epitome of everything good about the Jersey shore. There was a beach, of course, but there was also a boardwalk with rides, games, prizes, music, fun, and food. We'd go early and spend the whole day on the beach—blankets, umbrellas, and coolers with lunch and drinks packed to eat right on the sand. Near dinnertime, we'd pack it all up, load the car, and then shower and change in the boardwalk locker rooms. With hair still wet, we'd head to the food stands to eat something fried and greasy and, afterward, ride the rides and maybe try to win a big stuffed something at the arcade games. We'd stay way past dark, and oftentimes, I'd fall asleep on the way home.

My mother knew not to tell me too far in advance that we were going to Seaside. She'd tell me the night before, and inevitably, I'd be so excited I couldn't fall asleep. The anticipation of what was to come would bubble up inside me. Every time I closed my eyes, I'd see myself on the beach or on a fun ride or carrying a stuffed bear that was bigger than me. I'd be filled with the joy of anticipation long before we ever got to the beach.

Thinking back on those times of joyful anticipation made me think about the future and when I might have opportunity to experience that kind of joy and excitement again. And then it hit me! Shouldn't I be living every day with boundless, joyful anticipation? Aren't we awaiting the glorious return of the Messiah? I should be longing for that day and spilling over with joy every moment in anticipation of Christ's return.

Of course, Jesus may not return during my lifetime or yours. What is certain, though, is that we will one day see the face of our Savior. One day, we'll go home to be with Jesus. I can't think of anything better to joyfully anticipate than eternity in the presence of God. Paul knew it, too, and shared it with the church as he pressed toward the prize of living with Jesus forever.

May we live with Paul's eternal perspective as we wait with hearts full of joyful anticipation!

Creator God, help me to see the new thing You are doing. Keep my eyes fixed on Jesus, living always with an eternal perspective. Fill me with the joy of anticipating Christ's return. Amen.

Day 58

"If anyone comes to me and does not hate his own father and mother and wife and children and brothers and sisters, yes, and even his own life he cannot be my disciple . . . . So therefore, any one of you who does not renounce all that he has cannot be my disciple.

—Luke 14:26, 33

A Love Like That

NIKI

DOES JESUS REALLY WANT us to hate our families and ourselves? How can that be? He also told us to love even our enemies.

Moms and dads, do you remember feeling that overwhelming love at the first sight of your wrinkly little newborn? As a new young mom, that kind of love brought me to a place where I knew I would give my life to protect my children. As my babies grew, so did my love for them. I was a baby myself in those early years of motherhood, a "baby Christian."

During that time, I heard a sermon about loving God above everyone and everything. I thought to myself, *It's not possible for me to love anyone—even God—as much as I love these babies.* And I meant it. God had given me a precious gift in my two sons, and my full heart turned them into idols of my love.

This form of idolatry is what Jesus was warning against. He goes on to include everything else in the world we could possibly make into an idol of our hearts. God isn't telling us to hate our families and to hate the things He's given us as blessings to enjoy. Instead, He is telling us to *love Him* with our all—hearts, minds, spirits, bodies—and above every other person or thing.

I couldn't understand it as a new mom, but I do now. While I love my family with everything in me, my heart beats first and foremost for my Lord, my Savior, my King. My love for God grew as I came to know Him more intimately. My love for Him in no way lessens my love for my family. I love them deeply, but I love God more, and that is as it should be. God is love, and He created us to love Him. Only when we love God first are we able to love others the way He does. My family and yours need that kind of love from us—God first, every other person and blessing loved because of our love for Him.

The Tension

CONSTANCE

I DON'T BELIEVE JESUS MEANS for us to literally hate our family members or renounce all the material gifts we are blessed to have received. The story behind this challenging verse is deeper. I love my family, but they are not above my deeper love and desire to follow Jesus. When I responded to His call and received the greatest gift from the Giver of Life, my whole life changed. The ways I endeavor to love my family and those I come in contact with is the way Jesus loves me, sacrificially and unconditionally.

Earlier in Luke 14, Jesus told of a man who planned a banquet, but when the day arrived, many guests who had committed to coming to the celebration said they couldn't attend, giving excuses, such as family, farming, and livestock responsibilities. Yet, a lot of preparation and effort, along with anticipation, went into planning this party.

There are many instances in the New Testament when Jesus invited people to follow Him, especially after they had an interaction with Him. Instead, they, too, gave excuses why they couldn't leave their responsibilities (Luke 9:57–62).

Jesus uses the word "hate" to draw impassioned attention to the importance of being His disciple. After all, masses of people were flocking to Him wherever he went. They were willing to come to hear a sermon and see miracles performed, but would they have excuses when He asked them to become His disciples and carry the gospel worldwide? Sit with the tension of His words and allow the Spirit to speak to your heart.

To be His disciple, we must be committed to the work of the Kingdom and to Him above all else. The world needs Jesus. We're called to be imitators of our beloved Jesus who gave His life for us. We mustn't let anything take His place in our lives. Following Jesus wholeheartedly and in humility, even with those with whom we disagree, is the best choice.

I sometimes tend to make excuses as to why those who are hard to love don't deserve my kindness. Excuses are all around us. When He calls us to come follow Him, will we follow, or will we look for excuses?

Father, help me to always put You first in my heart.
Fill me with Your love, and help me to love those
You've given me with a love like Yours. Amen.

Day 59

But the Lord said to Samuel, "Do not look on his appearance
or on the height of his stature, because I have rejected
him. For the Lord sees not as man sees; man looks on the
outward appearance, but the Lord looks on the heart."

—*1 Samuel 16:7*

Never Give Up on Anyone

CONSTANCE

MANY YEARS AGO, SEBASTIAN was going through a challenging
and rebellious time, which deeply troubled both of us. As parents,
we pray for our children, try to impart godly wisdom, and hope they
choose God's best path. I knew my son's heart was sensitive and kind
and he loved God, but his actions reflected differently.

I was heartbroken for him. I searched for direction from God,
trying to find light in the darkness and truth for my soul. As I read
my Bible, God whispered, *I know his heart, Constance.*

I know Sebastian pretty well but certainly not as well as God. The
Word spoke to my spirit and mind, lightened my heart, and gave me
hope that God knows us and loves us more than we can comprehend.
He loves our children more than we're able to. I can give God my
desires and my heartache, leaving them at His feet.

People's lives are messy and complicated at times. Their outward
appearances and behaviors are often reflections of troubling inner
dramas. They need our understanding and God's grace, mercy, and

love. May we choose not to judge but instead pray for those who are being destructive (mostly to themselves), as God is working in all of our lives all of the time.

We aren't perfect. We're sinful humans on the way to becoming more Christ-like. We all experience struggles and mishaps, have wrong thoughts and habits—we are broken. Sometimes it's our upbringing, choices, or our waywardness. Even David was imperfect and committed despicable sins. But, he was humble and repentant, and God saw that David's heart was after His own.

Identity not Beauty

NIKI

IT SEEMS TO ME, GOD so often does things exactly the opposite of the world's ways. It's a good thing to keep in mind as we navigate life. The fact that God is most concerned with the condition of the heart is nothing new. It's a theme throughout all of Scripture. The things we think, say, and do come forth directly from our hearts. Though he was but a boy and small in stature, David was a man after God's own heart when He chose him to be king. But what about how we tend to evaluate other people, and ourselves?

God warned Samuel not to judge His choice of king by appearance, but the world is all about appearance. If we're not aware and careful, we can easily become caught up in image. This trap can be especially harmful for girls and women. From the time of birth, it seems, women are often valued most for their beauty. It's almost impossible not to fall into the trap of evaluating ourselves by how we look. Makeup is a multi-billion-dollar industry! There's nothing wrong with wearing makeup, styling our hair, and wearing fashionable clothes. The problem comes if it's in these things that we place our identity.

Have you ever caught yourself walking by a storefront window and watching your reflection as it goes by? Or how about quickly glancing in a mirror as you pass by? I have. I know it comes from insecurity in my appearance and is telling of the focus of my heart in those moments. But aging comes to all of us, and so beauty is only temporal. Just as I want to find my joy in something unchanging, something permanent, so too, I want to find my *identity* in the unchanging and permanent. That is most certainly not my face and body. The passing years teach that hard lesson. But when I find my identity in Jesus, nothing and no one can ever change it or take it from me.

So, what does it mean to find our identity in Jesus? It means wholly putting our trust in Him. It means surrendering all control to Him. It means when God looks at us, He sees the righteousness of Jesus because we've given Him our hearts and accepted His forgiveness. He sees us as never having sinned at all, just like Jesus. He sees us as His beloved sons and daughters, whom He loves with a love so great we can't fully comprehend it. May we allow Christ's holiness to cover us and to identify us, for now and forever. True beauty comes in belonging to Jesus and allowing the world to see it!

*Lord, have mercy on us. I give You my heart,
wholly and fully surrendered. Amen.*

Day 60

Whose Battle Is It?

NIKI

WHEN I WAS FIFTEEN, EIGHT YEARS into the powerlessness of sexual abuse, I felt completely without hope. I saw no way out and thought often about death being my only escape. Mired in feelings of hopelessness, one afternoon, I took a razor blade from the medicine cabinet in my bathroom. I looked at my face in the mirror as I held the blade and thought, *Today it can be over.* I hadn't written a note; I couldn't put the words on paper. I turned away from the mirror, climbed into the bathtub, sat down, and held the blade to my wrist. Tears trickled down my face. I feared the pain but not the dying. In those moments, I wanted to be dead. I sat that way for a long time, hoping to persuade myself to make the first cut. In the end, fear (and God, though I didn't yet know it) took hold of me and kept me from slicing that blade through my vein.

In 2 Chronicles 20, Jehoshaphat, Judah's king, faced three armies coming against him and leaving him feeling powerless against them. Though he was afraid, he was not without hope. All of Judah came together to seek the help of the Lord. When Jehoshaphat prayed for Judah and for God's deliverance, he acknowledged they didn't know what to do in the face of such a large and threatening enemy, but God did. And so they put their hope wholly in Him.

As Christ followers, we are *never* without hope. Even in the darkest, most evil circumstances, Christ is on our side. We always have reason to put our hope in Jesus. As Jehoshaphat ended his prayer, acknowledging Judah's weakness and God's strength, Jahaziel prophesied, "Thus says the Lord to you, 'Do not be afraid and do not be dismayed at this great horde, for the battle is not yours but God's'" (2 Chronicles 20:15b).

Jehoshaphat had the faith to believe God fights for His people. At fifteen, I didn't have that kind of faith, and it almost cost me my life. But God is good; He brought me through that dark period and pursued me even when I didn't know Him.

With your eyes on Him, trust God will fight for you, too.

I Survive; God Prevails, Always!

CONSTANCE

I ONCE WORKED AS A FRONT DESK attendant for a hotel. At that time, our family was experiencing a challenging situation that required our complete attention. I was also attending community college and had just relocated to Charleston from Maryland.

One morning, a hotel guest approached me, "Do you have a gym?" My response, "I'm sure we do; what department does he work in?" An hour later, another guest requested that I make a copy for him. I responded, "You can get a coffee at Starbucks downstairs." Both times, my coworker rescued me and later asked, "Are you okay, Constance?" Obviously, I wasn't, but I managed to finish the day without another silly comment. Extended times of emotional distress and worry are harmful for the mind as well as the body. My issue wasn't a hearing deficit but an overly stress-filled mind.

I was doing my best to trust God, but the anxiety was taking a toll on my physical and mental health. I didn't know how things would work out or what I would do if they didn't. Hopelessness and worry were taking my mind captive, and I had no control of the outcome. Some days, my prayer was one word—"Jesus." Other days, I laid on our window seat for hours yearning for peace. I looked to God, but I couldn't hear Him. We often don't know what to do, but we can keep our eyes on the One who does, even when the circumstances feel otherwise.

We ultimately got through that situation with a result not nearly as bad as imagined. God handled the outcome as only He can.

Trust is an interesting action. We trust without thinking that cars will stop at red lights, and the electricity will work when we flip the switch. Trusting in the Creator of the universe is often the hardest, but He is the best Person in Whom to place our trust. God is present in our pain, in our most glorious moments, and in everything in between. When you don't know what to do, keep your eyes on Him. Trust Him. He will carry you.

Holy God, how many battles have You fought for me, delivering me without me even aware? Thank You for Your loving kindness and tender mercy. Help me to always keep my eyes on You. Amen.

Day 61

*But godliness with contentment is great gain, for
we brought nothing into the world, and we cannot
take anything out of the world. But if we have food
and clothing, with these we will be content.*

—*1 Timothy 6:6–8*

Time to Dance to a New Beat

CONSTANCE

SOME TIME AGO, I READ Marie Kondo's book, *The Life-Changing
Magic of Tidying Up*. I was motivated to begin the journey of declut-
tering and thus began a weeklong, life-changing experience. I emptied
bookcases, kitchen cabinets, and closets in every room of my home
and garage. After purging, I slowly refilled those areas through the
filter of necessity and bringing joy. The endeavor was challenging but
fun. It was freeing to let go of things I didn't use and encouraging to
donate books, clothes, and kitchen utensils.

Sitting on my sofa in my newly transformed living room, I felt
calm and relaxed. I loved the way it looked. Surprised by my reactions,
I contemplated implementing Kondo's concept in my personal life,
being more selective in what I allow in. What are the things that
bring me joy? Am I allowing too many activities to clutter my time,
sacrificing relationships, especially with God?

Jesus prioritized time alone with His Father. He made time to minister to people and commune with family, friends, and His disciples.

I presume He was able to sustain his physical and spiritual health by not being concerned with possessions, allowing Him to focus on what is most important—the Father's will.

Culture encourages us to work hard so we can own more, fill our calendars with activities, engage in superficial or obligatory relationships, all with no time to spare. Perhaps God desires a simpler life for us, one of humility, helping others, and having meaningful relationships. What do we need to purge so we can have quality relationships with Jesus and with others?

Ms. Kondo's book made me realize I could live with less and be happy. Jesus showed us what is important in life—loving Him and living a simple life. In his letter to Timothy, Paul encourages us with the truth that godliness leads to contentment. Living a life of gratitude for what we have is important. How can you live a more simplified life, one that allows time with our Father, and time for the ones who bring joy and love to your life?

What's in All Those Boxes Anyway?

NIKI

WHILE PREPARING FOR OUR MOST recent move, Joe and I trudged to our cluttered basement to sort through the many boxes stored there. Several of the boxes were still packed from our move nine years prior. Many times over those nine years, I commented to Joe that we obviously didn't need whatever was in those boxes since we'd gone all those years without missing their contents. I finally convinced him to look through the boxes instead of moving them to our next soon-to-be-cluttered basement or garage.

We live in a culture of excess—everywhere we look, we're told to get more, more, more—when all we need is to know Jesus and to trust God's provision for our other needs. God is not impressed by what we own and, therefore, neither should we be. He cares about the condition of our hearts, our character, and our relationship with Him. God cares about godliness. These are the things we'll take to heaven with us, so these are the things we should spend time cultivating.

The dictionary defines godliness as "divine, pious, devout; being blessed, holy, sacred." All of these attributes encompassing godliness are characteristics we can never achieve on our own. How can I be holy or divine when I have a human heart beating within me? But isn't it like God to provide all we need to grow toward godliness? Paul knew it by evidence of our key verses. God already has given us all we need to grow into godliness through coming to know Jesus Christ personally. A close relationship with our Lord and Savior is where we find contentment.

Joe and I did open all of those boxes in our basement. We threw away or donated more things than we kept. We took photos of the many things our hearts ached at letting go. It was a good compromise.

We came with nothing into this world, and we'll leave with nothing, except the most important thing—our relationship with the One who gave us everything.

Father, show me how to eliminate the unnecessary, so I can enjoy the necessary that brings joy and peace to my life. Amen.

Day 62

*But our citizenship is in heaven, and from it we await
a Savior, the Lord Jesus Christ, who will transform
our lowly body to be like his glorious body, by the power
that enables him to subject all things to himself.*

—Philippians 3:20–21

Oh! My Aching . . .

NIKI

I'M IN THE TWILIGHT SEASON of my life, nearing the end of my seventh decade. My body often aches, and I'm intimately familiar with its slow decay. Even still, I'm experiencing elder age to be a beautiful time.

As one ages, what others think about you matters less and less. There's peace in letting all of that angst go. There's also freedom, hopefully, from the time restraints of working a full-time job and raising a family. This season of life allows me to spend unhurried time with Jesus every morning. Then, there are the grandchildren!

But there's one blessing that surprised me. My own slowly failing body reminds me, as each day passes, I'm that much closer to being home with Jesus where I've been meant to be from the beginning. God always intended for us to live face to face with Him forever.

Like everything in this world, these lowly bodies are temporary. One day, when Jesus returns, He'll give us glorious bodies like His—bodies that will never die, ache, wrinkle, or decay. Our new bodies will fit us perfectly for all of eternity. It's impossible to even imagine the glory and the glorious bodies that await us in heaven!

In the meantime, with every ache or pain, diagnosis, or extra pound, I'm reminded this body is mine for only a short time. The aging of my earthly body truly brings me joy as it reminds me Jesus is preparing my place in heaven. I long to be there with Him.

The joy in this season of life is all about perspective. We can let our pains and increasing frailties bring us sorrow or bring us joy.

Passing Through to Glory

CONSTANCE

WE DON'T NEED TO TRAVEL outside America to experience huge cultural shifts. Consider the southern states verses northern states, the Hawaiian Islands or Alaska, or even the Appalachian Mountains. All have different lifestyles, customs, and traditions. I imagine we could find ourselves feeling disconnected or uncomfortable at times in those unfamiliar places. They're not like home.

We're blessed to live in the United States, although we aren't so united at times. Some days, everything appears "out of sorts." I was having one of those days recently. My heart was screaming with unmet desires, heart wounds not yet healed, abandonment issues, all of them crushing me in despair and hopelessness. I wanted someone to rescue me from the daily pressures of months of advocating for Carroll in medical establishments; I needed to be heard and respected.

I've noticed that many of the same scenarios of chaos and pain in our world also appear throughout Scripture. Humans have made a mess of things ever since Eden! Could our hearts be yearning for the Garden of Eden that God intended for us before sin entered the world? It was to be our home with God, walking in the cool of the day.

On difficult days, I need to remember that we're just passing through. Our citizenship, as Paul says, is in heaven. One day, there will be a new earth without suffering. We eagerly await the return of our Lord and the promise of a glorious body, immortal and sinless. One day, perhaps in our lifetime, we will be filled with all the fullness of God (Ephesians 3:19). Accepting Jesus as our Lord and Savior, His resurrection, and promise to return is what secures our citizenship in the household of God, no longer strangers in a foreign land.

Father God, thank You for the many days You've already given me in this earthly body. Help me use each remaining day to honor You and bring You praise. Thank You for Your promise of my glorious body to come! Amen.

Day 63

For the Lord spoke thus to me with his strong hand upon me,
and warned me not to walk in the way of this people.

—Isaiah 8:11

Do You Need a Sabbatical?

CONSTANCE

FOR TEN MONTHS I DECIDED to keep the television off—no cable or nightly news. My months were void of the "news regurgitation loop" of someone else's opinions and the constant dehumanization of mankind. There were conspiracies circulating, fake news, and censorship of opposing opinions on mostly everything. I was disenchanted by all media outlets and even certain religious organizations.

As I prayed for our country during this time, I invited the Holy Spirit to teach me how to live in this world. We're all susceptible to worldly influence, but I wanted to bless those I met with joy. I needed it myself. Rather than join the darkness, we can be the light of Jesus. We can be envoys of love, not participants in lies and hate. God showed me, perhaps because I wasn't participating in the never-ending dialog that was going nowhere, what I couldn't see before—the spiritual warfare raging all around me. There's a battle for the soul going on—the spirit of the world versus the Spirit of God.

Maybe you, like me, need a hiatus from whatever is pulling your attention away from God. Jesus lovingly sent the Holy Spirit for us. The spirit of this world models deception, division, immorality, hate, and every evil thing. The Spirit of God is truth, love, joy, goodness, faithfulness, and a multitude of other beautiful, uplifting attributes. We need the Holy Spirit, not the spirit of the world.

Can you receive the Lord's word in Isaiah 8:12–13a for yourself? "Do not call conspiracy all that this people calls conspiracy, and do not fear what they fear, nor be in dread. But the Lord of hosts, him you shall honor as holy."

Running Rodents

NIKI

THERE IS A MISCONCEPTION about lemmings, those little rodents. It goes like this. Lemmings have a herd mentality when it comes to migration (true), and when one starts running, they all will follow (true), even to the point of mass suicide (not true). If they should run off a cliff to their death, it's not because they have a death wish. It's a result of their migratory behavior. Thus, the misconception. There are no suicidal lemmings. They all do run, however. When one starts the flow, they go.

Joe and I were recently in Italy for the first time, celebrating several milestones. We traveled often by train, with our first train ride leaving Rome. We arrived early to the massive station, checked the electronic boards, and found we would be leaving from Platform 1. I showed our tickets to the guy manning the gate to be sure we were in the right place. He barely glanced and said yes. On the platform, we waited and waited some more. There was no train.

All of a sudden, we saw many people running *fast* past us down the platform. We looked at each other in confusion, and then I looked up and saw a sign saying Platform 1E is way down the tracks to where this crowd is running. And there's a train down there! What do we do? Start running with them, of course. I felt a possible imminent heart attack as I dragged my fifty-pound suitcase after me and sprinted fast. When I could go no farther, Joe ran on to where a conductor stood outside the train. He showed him our tickets. He shook his head and said, "This is Platform 1 East, not 1." Back to Platform 1 we trudged. There still was no train at Platform 1 because unbeknownst to us, they had changed our train to Platform 11. And so we had missed it. Though flustered, sweating, and out of breath, we easily rebooked for just a few Euro. Once safely on the train, Joe commented how we had acted just like lemmings!

There can be danger in following the crowd. We can be easily in-fluenced by the company we keep. In Isaiah 8, God warned Isaiah to follow only Him and not walk (or run like a lemming) in the way of the people around him. We're *in* the world but *not of* the world (John 17:14–19). How? By coming to know God in a heart-changing way, by staying close to Him through personal time with Him in His Word.

We learned a good lesson about following the crowd in Rome. Let's not be lemmings in spiritual situations either. Come to know Jesus for yourself. His character is infinite, as is His love.

Holy Father, I ask for wisdom and discernment
in my life to know what is true. Keep me running
after only You all the days of my life. Amen.

Day 64

Count it all joy, my brothers, when you meet trials of various kinds,
for you know that the testing of your faith produces steadfastness.

—*James 1:2–3*

To Whom Are You Tethered?

NIKI

NOT LONG AGO, I WALKED through the most painful experience of my life. Hurting my child hurts me like nothing else can. At the beginning of that season of suffering, I questioned whether my faith would stand firm. Early on, I met with a friend and told her my family's story through tears of heartbreak, sharing the greatest fear I've ever known. She let me pour out every raw emotion that consumed me. Finally, she said, "Niki, your Anchor will hold." I'll never forget those words.

James, the Lord's half-brother, is not one to mince words. It's one of the things I like most about his letter. He writes clearly and to the point. His clear, say-what-you-mean style starts right here in the beginning verses of his letter. We can count on our faith being tested through trials.

Steadfast means immovable, and that's what trials can do for our faith. It's important to remember it's the standing firm in our faith that builds endurance, not the trial itself. If we run to God instead of away from Him in a hard season, our faith is cemented into our Rock, our Anchor. It will hold through the fiercest of storms. Trials will either make you better—growing a stronger, deeper faith, or bitter—turning from and blaming God.

Some translations of James 1:3 use the word patience instead of steadfastness. Both words are appropriate to faith in times of trial. When we're suffering, we want rescue now. Waiting on God's timing is difficult, to put it mildly. Patience is hardest when you need it the most. Trusting God's timing in suffering grows patience like nothing else can.

A patient and steadfast faith is a priceless blessing God brings out of trials. It is a faith of spiritual growth that leads to spiritual maturity. It's the good happening in our hearts, even in the midst of suffering, and it's a reason for joy. God uses our lifetimes to make us more like Jesus, and He knows best how to accomplish that purpose. May we continue to put our faith in Him as He allows into our lives what He knows will grow us and draw us near to Him. May our dependence on God alone be our strength in times of trouble, for our faith tethers us to the most durable, immovable Anchor. And Jesus will hold.

Training to Reign

CONSTANCE

OPTING TO LINGER IN MY CAR in front of the post office entrance for a couple of minutes while my guy went inside to deposit letters, I heard a thump while waiting but surmised a squirrel was scrambling around underneath. Aware my husband was taking longer than expected, I drove forward a few feet, intending to take a parking space. I quickly realized I had driven over something. Glancing in the rearview mirror, I noticed people anxiously vacating their vehicles, as did I. I gasped as my stomach clenched. Unbeknownst to me, Carroll had fainted while approaching the car, thus the thud I heard minutes before. His feet were under the car in direct line with my tires. I had run over Carroll's feet with my SUV!

Finally coming to, he stood up, claiming he was fine, until he wasn't! We went to the hospital and received confirmation that his feet were badly bruised and swollen but not broken. In the midst of this unfolding drama, I felt my life as I knew it was over. My first thought was, "I killed my husband!" I couldn't shake the shame I felt in having run over Carroll with my car. I felt desperately out of sorts and emotionally drained.

At any given moment, hope can slide away and dread jump in. Emotions often drive our reactions to our circumstances. Jesus understands the dynamics behind our tendency to be emotional. He had opportunities for reactions—turning tables over in the temple (anger), seeking solitude when John the Baptist was killed (sadness), feeling deeply moved when He saw the grief of Mary and Martha over the death of their brother, Lazarus (grief).

Paraphrasing what David so succinctly penned in Psalm 23, though we walk through the valley of the shadow of death at times, we fear no evil, for His protection, direction, and shepherding bring us comfort. We often don't see so clearly in the "now" moment, but reflecting back over our past, we can more easily see what we couldn't before. I couldn't see what had happened that morning at the post office until I looked in the rearview mirror. God is committed to our growth and well-being. He has given us strength to stand through every situation we've encountered. He is faithful.

Carroll and I still laugh about that day at the post office. It took a few hours for me to regain my equanimity but weeks before his feet were healed. Our current challenges provide growth and reliance on God in *all* things. Let's approach each day with the mindset that God knows our stories, and we can rest in His capable hands.

Father, You alone are the One I run to in my suffering.
Help me to rest in Your shepherding and protection,
knowing You are holding my hand along the way. Use these
seasons to more deeply tether my faith to Jesus. Amen.

Day 65

And God said to him, "Because you have . . . asked for yourself
understanding to discern what is right . . . . Behold, I give
you a wise and discerning mind, so that none like you has
been before you and none like you shall arise after you."

—1 Kings 3:11–12

The Dream That Changes Everything

CONSTANCE

I HARBOR "HOLY JEALOUSY" OF SOLOMON'S conversation with
God in a dream that eventually came true. Imagine God saying to
you, "Ask what I shall give you" (1 Kings 3:5). What would your list
include? Solomon's response didn't include riches, long life, status, or
power. Instead, he desired the understanding and discernment necessary to govern God's people well. Solomon perceived the enormous
responsibility that lay ahead of him when he uttered to God, "I am
but a little child" (1 Kings 3:7).

God's response was generous and extravagant. God granted Solomon
a wise and discerning mind, and He rewarded him with riches and
honor. He also promised Solomon length of days if he would walk in
God's ways and keep His laws and commandments, just as his father,
David, had done. Questing for God's perfect will, asking heartfelt
questions, yielding our ears to hear, our eyes to see, and our minds to
understand will lead to hearts surrendered to God and His presence.

Many of my prayers have been answered; yet I still wait with hope in faith for unanswered prayers. God wants to answer our prayers, but He also desires relationship. Prayer is about connection, a covenant of love with Jesus. Jesus perfectly described the covenant of love He desires with us. As His Father loved Him, so He loves us.

Prayer is the act of clearing ourselves of the distractions in our lives to be alone with God. Life has always been about love—God's love for you, me, and all of humanity.

A Word to the Wise

NIKI

WITHOUT THINKING LONGER THAN A SECOND, how would you answer God if He asked, "What do you want? Ask, and I will give it to you!" What's the first thing that came to mind?

Can you see God's infinite wisdom in the question he asked Solomon? The answer coming without thinking too much is a revelation, an opening of the door into the condition of one's heart. While Solomon did ask for something for himself—wisdom—he asked for the benefit of the entire body of God's chosen people. He was a new king and understood his weaknesses and limitations in governing the people. "It pleased the Lord that Solomon had asked this" (1 Kings 3:10).

What does your answer to God's question reveal about your heart? In His three-year ministry, Christ often spoke of the heart. In the King James Version of the Bible, the heart is mentioned eight hundred twenty-six times![1] When God speaks of something even once, it has

---

1 Strong, James, *Strong's Exhaustive Concordance of the Bible,* Hendrickson Academic, Updated Edition, January 1, 2009.

importance. What does eight hundred twenty-six times lead you to believe about the importance of our hearts to the Lord? Everything we think, say, and do flows from the heart. The heart cradles our character, and it's our character that goes with us into eternity.

Does your answer to "What do you want?" come first in your prayers? If your answer would please the Lord and it's at the top of your without-even-thinking list, it should have a prominent place in your conversations with Him. Thanksgiving, praise, cares, and desires, God wants us to bring it all to Him.

Examining the heart is not a "one and done." We're constantly exposed to things, either on purpose or not, that affect the state of our hearts. But, thank God, we have an Advocate who is in the business of heart change. May we fully entrust the condition of our hearts into the hands of the Holy Spirit, praying always for God's will to be done.

Most Gracious Father, grant me an understanding heart and discernment between good and evil, so I may be wise in every decision. Amen.

Day 66

*"If this be so, our God whom we serve is able to deliver us from
the burning fiery furnace, and he will deliver us out of your hand,
O king. But if not, be it known to you, O king, that we will not
serve your gods or worship the golden image that you have set up."*

—Daniel 3:17–18

But If Not . . .

NIKI

SHADRACH, MESHACH, AND ABEDNEGO faced death by being
thrown into a furnace heated seven times hotter than usual. They could
save themselves by bowing down and worshiping the golden statue
that King Nebuchadnezzar constructed and which he proclaimed
all would worship whenever they heard music. They sealed their fate
by their refusal.

These three men trusted God could and would deliver them. But
the amazing words they spoke to the king were, "But if not . . . ."
Their faith in God would stand even if He didn't deliver them from
the fire. That's the faith I want to have!

If you spend some time in the Bible, you'll see God makes many
promises to those who love and follow Him. One promise He doesn't
make, however, is the promise of a good or happy outcome to a trying
circumstance or season. It's in this unknown that God often chooses
to grow and mature our faith to a "but if not" kind of faith.

The unknown outcome to a suffering season isn't a place we'd choose to be, but it's a place we can be thankful for. It's in this place that our trust in God's goodness is put to the test. It's in this place, we can draw nearer to God as we rely on Him. It's in this place, we can come to know our faith will stand firm on the Lord. Our Anchor will hold us, even if God doesn't bring us through with the outcome we're desperately praying for. It's in this place, we can grow in understanding that God's will for us is always our best-case scenario.

With faith like Shadrach, Meshach, and Abednego, we can continue to hope and pray fervently, knowing God will carry us through any outcome. He is with us; He is for us; His will is what's best, even in situations that make no sense to our limited human understanding. God is God, and we aren't. Thank God!

A Hot Oven Burns Sometimes

CONSTANCE

IN AMERICA WE HAVE RELIGIOUS freedom, but in some countries, Christians face death for not renouncing their faith in God. Their sacrificial obedience is inspiring, and it stirs us to ponder our own convictions when faced with persecution.

Shadrach, Meshach, and Abednego were united in their refusal to obey the king's order to bow down to his gods and the golden image. They wholeheartedly believed the God they served was able to deliver them from the fiery furnace and out of the king's hand. But even if God didn't save them from the fire, they were holding onto their faith in Him. Their noncompliance to the king's orders stirred up his fury, and into the furnace they went.

The king was astonished when he saw four persons walking around in the furnace. Immediately and without doubt, he recognized the true God and set the formerly bound men free from the fire. His life was changed that day, and I'm sure others were as well.

How confident are we that our God will deliver us in our greatest need? It's easy to become disillusioned when things look bleak, but that is the time to press in and recall God's history of faithfulness. Your miracle may be just around the corner!

We aren't alone when going through difficult seasons. During an extended season of challenges that dragged on for months, I attended church weekly. My small group was my anchor. Several friends commented about our persevering faith and how it was an inspiration for them. Not only did their words encourage me, because I was unaware of having any influence, but I was also deeply moved that our faith was meaningful to them. Life shared in relationship when facing our own fiery furnaces is critical. We need each other; we are the body of Christ.

Today many of our Christian beliefs are threatened, and our faith is challenged by the culture in which we live. It's painful and uncomfortable at times to stand up for our principles and beliefs, but it's empowering to see God work on our behalf. Our faith *is* worth dying for. Jesus thought so when He died so we might live.

Father, bring me to a faith that trusts in You no matter the outcome of my circumstances. Help me to have faith in You and Your goodness. Amen.

Day 67

And he said, "Abba, Father, all things are possible for you. Remove this cup from me. Yet not what I will, but what you will."

—Mark 14:36

The Garden of Pain and Surrender

CONSTANCE

MY CHURCH PLANNED A TRIP to Israel, and I had always wanted to go to the land of the Bible. I registered, but as the trip came closer, I wasn't sure I'd be able to follow through with my plans because of circumstances out of my control. I felt a deep-seated need for this trip, and thankfully, everything did align for me to travel.

Toward the end of our tour, we went to Gethsemane, the garden where Jesus went to pray prior to His arrest and crucifixion. In this beautiful garden, full of foliage and olive trees, we each found a place to reflect. I began experiencing the heaviness of Jesus' heart and words as He prayed earnestly and in agony for what was before Him in the coming days, and I was overcome by emotion. My tears fell into the small wooden chalice I was holding. Nothing compares to the burden Jesus was carrying when He asked God to "remove this cup" from Him, but at that moment and place in the garden, His prayer was my request to the Father as well.

I wasn't ready to return to the unending responsibilities of advocate and caregiver I had been experiencing during the prior six months. I was tender and exhausted. But I heard Jesus' prayer to His Father in my heart, ". . . not what I will, but what you will." I continued to allow the Spirit to flood me with love as I poured out my heart to my Father in complete surrender to His will that day in Gethsemane. I soon knew I could go home. It was yielding my will to the Father's will and acknowledging within my soul that I would be able to do whatever was asked of me because I had Jesus.

The moment we realize, as Jesus did, that God's plan is best, we willingly give it all to Him. Friends, there is freedom and peace in surrender! No matter what is going on in our lives, His love carries us through difficult and challenging trials and seasons of life.

Are you in a season you wish you could escape? Remind yourself that Jesus understands, and the Holy Spirit is your Comforter. Surrender isn't easy, but it is the best way to live free from fear and anxiety. Trust your Father and trust His plan. He adores you.

Teach Me to Pray . . . and to Trust

NIKI

WHEN I WAS A NEW BELIEVER, I never volunteered to be the one to pray aloud in a group. It made me nervous. I loved listening to others pray and especially loved when someone would whisper, "Yes" or "Amen" during another's prayer. I imagined how affirming hearing those soft words would be. As time went on, I became more comfortable praying aloud. It helped not to focus on the people and what they would think of my words but on the God to whom I prayed.

I longed to pray together with Joe, but after many years, it still had not happened. We both believed it would be awkward, and our prayers were too private to share. How could I pray aloud for him if I'm praying with him? Those feelings vanished when a life situation brought us both to our knees. All of a sudden, praying together brought us comfort instead of awkwardness. Since that moment four years ago, we pray together every night before bed. And we do pray aloud for each other. I love to hear my husband's heart in his prayers for me.

While I love to pray with Joe, and believe it's important, the time I spend alone with my Father in prayer is my secret treasure. Jesus is always our perfect example, including in prayer. He often went away to a place by Himself to pray. If Jesus needed to be alone with His Father, then so do we.

In today's verse, Jesus acknowledged God's omnipotence (can do anything), and He acknowledged God's omniscience (knows all things) by asking for God's will to supersede His own. He knew the resulting goodness that would come from submission and that God would be glorified through it. When we come to trust and love God with everything we are, our prayers can begin to reflect Christ's prayers.

God is always good, His heart is for our ultimate good, and He loves us with an unfailing love. May we find time every day to be alone with our Father and rest in His capable hands. Let's pray!

Father, I come to You to submit to Your will, not mine.
Help me to have a surrendered heart always. Amen.

Day 68

"Then we turned and journeyed into the wilderness in the direction of the Red Sea, as the Lord told me. And for many days we traveled around Mount Seir. Then the Lord said to me, 'You have been traveling around this mountain country long enough.'"

—Deuteronomy 2:1–3a

Maybe Later . . .

NIKI

I WORKED IN AN OFFICE for twenty years. First as a legal secretary, then an administrative assistant, then an office manager, and finally, an assistant editor. If you had passed by my desk in all four of those offices, you would have noticed that my desktop usually looked like no one ever used it. I worked under the philosophy of "handle it once." Whatever crossed my desk, whether from a coworker, my boss, or the incoming mail, I tried my best to handle it immediately. If it needed to be filed, I filed it right away. If it needed a letter or an email, I took care of it right then. If it needed a phone call, I called. One thing no one could accuse me of was being a procrastinator. That philosophy carried over into my home life as much as possible. I tackled the thing I most dreaded first, saving the more pleasant tasks as my reward.

Procrastination reminds me of the Israelites when God told them to enter the Promised Land. Having scouted the land and its inhabitants, they decided not to move. Later, when they realized their disobedience, they moved forward but found that God was no longer with them. And so, in Deuteronomy 2, they find themselves unable to enter the land because of their earlier disobedience. Delayed obedience is disobedience. God waited forty years for that generation to die off in the wilderness before He moved with His people into the Promised Land. Obedience is important to God.

We're human, though. God never expects perfection from us. He knows our weaknesses; He created us. It's His provision of grace and power that carry us through, giving us what we need to be obedient. God never leaves us on our own.

Procrastination is a burden that feels heavier over time. When it's linked to God's commands or calling for us, it's more than heavy. It's disobedience. God's desire is always for our good, and Christ's power rests upon us. When we sense God calling us to move, it's time to move!

Wander for Wonder

CONSTANCE

A CLOSE FRIEND AND I MEET once a year at her family's mountain cottage in North Carolina. In the mountains, God always provides generous times for hiking and dining at our favorite cafe, but He also provides a beautiful dance of listening and speaking, learning and relearning, both for us with each other and with Him.

One morning, I went for a walk alone in the neighborhood. I walked up and down the hilly roads, enjoying the views and the exercise. I felt sure I knew the way back. Things looked familiar, but I soon realized I was lost. I kept walking, trusting I would find the house. After five miles and several hours, I came through the door to greet my concerned friend.

My four hours of wandering was a mere fraction of what the Israelites experienced in the wilderness. They wandered for forty years. Because of their fear of the unknown and their disobedience, God prevented them from entering the Promised Land. So, they roamed, dependent on God for water and food. When the next generation finally entered the land flowing with milk and honey, they must have been surprised. The new land wasn't that far from the desert where they had been wandering. They had missed so much, and yet they gained valuable lessons in the waiting (Deuteronomy 1 and 2). Their unwillingness to trust God led them to a place of extreme conditions and isolation where they learned about God's faithfulness and provision.

Do you get sidetracked in areas of fear and struggle? Is the yearning of your heart leading you to fields of green, along the rivers of life, through the valleys of forgiveness and acceptance of yourself and others? It might be time to reignite your curiosity about God and His love for you. I love walking for curiosity's sake, mindless at times, but often in deep meditation with God, praying and worshiping. I want that same blessing for you!

A sign hangs in my home—"Not All Who Wander Are Lost." Not only does it remind me of our "friends' weekend," but it also reminds me that with God, we can never be lost. His Spirit will always guide us home.

Lord God, help me to never wait when it comes to You.
Help me now to do the good works You've prepared for me
to do. Let my wandering paths lead me to You. Amen.

Day 69

And Gideon said to him, "Please, my Lord, if the Lord is with us, why then has all this happened to us?"

—Judges 6:13a

O, Mighty Man and Woman of Valor

CONSTANCE

I HAVE WALKED THROUGH SITUATIONS God could have prevented. However, the priceless wisdom received because I leaned into God's presence enabled me to prevail through many seemingly impossible circumstances. How have you experienced God in situations you thought would go differently?

When God told Gideon He would be with him and then proclaimed he was a mighty man of valor, it seems Gideon had difficulty receiving those words. He questioned why God Himself didn't save Israel from the Midianites. Gideon wanted God to fix the situation without him needing to go into battle. But God wanted Gideon to experience something that would change his life. Initially, thousands of men wanted to fight against the Midianites, but God whittled them down to three hundred who went to battle alongside Gideon. Gideon defended Israel as if the Midianites were a single man and saw the Almighty as his protector and defender. Certainly this was a battle Gideon would never forget—the Lord was on his side.

I'm reminded of young David, a shepherd boy, who stood firmly before Goliath, the Philistine, and proclaimed he was coming in the name of the God of Israel. Confident in his Lord and, I might add, in his own ability to sling a rock and hit his target, David took down Goliath, who was clothed with a sword, spear, and javelin. When the army of the Philistines saw their hero defeated, they retreated. Imagine the confidence of David compared to Gideon.

God can do what He wishes, but often, He wants to do the unimaginable in and through us. David knew who the Almighty was, but Gideon wasn't sure at first. Gideon thrived once he trusted God with his circumstances. God wants to display the miraculous through us, as we walk through hard situations beyond our control. Place your confidence in the Lord. When God doesn't respond as you had hoped, He could be wanting to do something more purposeful in your life—always with Him by your side.

God loves you! He will never leave you. Trust Him today and every day in all things. He is your protector. He is fighting your battles and enabling you to stand faithful in His strength.

Why Me?

NIKI

WHY ME? MOST OF US HAVE ASKED this question at some point in our lives. It's the first thing that comes to mind in a season of suffering. If we only knew why something was happening, maybe we'd be better able to stand up under it, pain and all. Gideon wanted to know why, too, but he also questioned how God could even allow the pain and suffering he and the Israelites were experiencing at the hands of the Midianites.

One thing I've come to realize through times of suffering is God doesn't owe us an explanation. Look at Job. All through Job's unbearable suffering, God never tells him why it's happening. Even after God gives Job back more than he had lost, God doesn't give him the reason why it happened. "How unsearchable are his judgments and how inscrutable his ways! 'For who has known the mind of the Lord, or who has been his counselor?'" (Romans 11:33b–34). Once I understood that God didn't owe me an explanation, I started asking a better question: "Why *not* me?" Or even better, "What do You want me to learn here, Lord?"

God is sovereign, and there is something He wants us to learn in every season of suffering. The "good" God promises to bring from working all things together for the good of those who love Him (Romans 8:28) might not look like we expect. He doesn't promise only happy outcomes to hard situations, but He does promise to bring some kind of benefit. In my experience, that benefit has most often been in a change in my own heart, a new nearness to God, hearing His voice in unexpected ways, experiencing His presence like never before.

There's so much about God we don't and can't understand, but He's given us all we need to come to know Him in ways that change us from the inside out. Spend time in Scripture. Ask Him for insight into what you read. God desires to be known. We may never know why He does some things the way He does, but if you come to know Him intimately through His Word, you'll know all you need to love Him. God is a good, good Father, One to be trusted even when we can't understand.

Holy Father, help my unbelief. Expand my heart to trust and my spirit to believe You are always with me. May I never resist the struggles but walk through them with Your guidance and protection. Amen.

Day 70

*And he said to me, "It is done! I am the Alpha and the
Omega, the beginning and the end. To the thirsty I will give
from the spring of the water of life without payment."*

—Revelation 21:6

Jesus Paid It All—Once
and Forevermore

NIKI

PEOPLE HAVE DIFFERING OPINIONS about tattoos, but I've wanted
one my entire life. I hesitated, though, because I couldn't envision a
design I'd want deeply enough to have permanently marked on my
body. By the time I was sixty-two years old, I finally knew the tattoo I
wanted, and I went for it. I joked with the artist about the likelihood
of being his oldest client getting her first tattoo, but I walked out
of the tattoo parlor with Christ's last words, "It is finished" (John
19:30), along with a tiny cross, marked permanently on the inside of
my right wrist.

Having come of age in a works-based religion, once I knew better, I wanted a constant reminder that Jesus finished the work of
my salvation on the cross. There is nothing else to be done except
to believe in Him and accept His freely given gift. In Revelation, at
the end of the story of humanity as we know it, Jesus declares the
very same words, "It is done!" (The New Living Translation says, "It
is finished!" in both John and Revelation.) From beginning to end,

Jesus takes on the responsibility of providing everything we need to be with Him forever in paradise. He is the Alpha and the Omega, and everything in between.

All three Persons of the Triune God have an essential role in our salvation. God the Father loves us enough to have sent His Beloved Son to earth to rescue and redeem us. Jesus took on the sin and punishment of all of humanity—the very wrath of God—to reconcile us to the Father. The Holy Spirit, in the here and now, guides, directs, strengthens, and prays for us in ways we don't even know we need.

Is there something that might help remind you that Jesus has done all that needs to be done for you to be with Him now and to live with Him in heaven forever? It doesn't have to be something as drastic as a tattoo. Maybe it's a necklace or a bracelet or a ring or something else that has personal significance to you and your relationship with the Lord. God knew we'd need reminders. (See Joshua 4:5–7, 21–22, and 1 Samuel 7:12.) I love that I now have a reminder that brings my mind and heart back to Jesus every time I see it. It is finished.

It Is Done!

CONSTANCE

I HAVE BEEN THE RESPONSIBLE gal for most of my life. To be responsible, I had to be in control. When I was in control, things were done properly and timely, but it came at a cost—anxiety and fatigue. What if we were to learn sooner rather than later that the entirety of our lives would be easier, and most likely better, if we surrendered control to the One who created us? I decided I must yield control of my life to God. Surrendering and releasing what I'm holding tightly (then realizing wasn't important anyway) was my first step. I wanted to be happy! With God in control, He gave me joy, a gift of the Holy Spirit, and then prompted me to begin sharing it with others out of the overflow in my heart and life.

If Jesus said, "It is done," then we can say it, too. What does that statement mean for us? Jesus, who has held this universe together from the beginning, can certainly hold our lives together. We can say we are done with the things holding us too tightly to the world. We can say yes to the gift Jesus has for us—peace through surrender.

Remember the story of the Samaritan woman at the well? It was difficult for her to understand that Jesus was asking her to give over control of her life and become a partaker of the living water He was offering, which brings eternal life.

Water is crucial to our existence and has always been a symbol for life. Jesus emphatically says that anyone who believes He is who He says He is—the Son of God—will have rivers of living water flowing from their hearts. The living water is free to all who ask and believe.

Are we accessing the blessings God has for us now while living in the midst of the very real juxtaposition of life—the wonder and the difficulty? Since Eden, we have shared responsibility with God over the welfare of His creation. He gave us authority in the first book of the Bible. In the last book, Jesus said, "It is done." What Jesus began, Jesus has finished—the making of all things new. We have hope in that reality and trust in the One who proclaims it. Allow your heart to become the dwelling place of God, surrender control to Him, and receive from the spring of life. Be thirsty for Him!

Most Holy Father, thank You for Jesus and for the gift of the Holy Spirit. May I never forget what You have done for me. Help me to create space in my heart for You to dwell. Amen.

Day 71

Out of the depths I cry to you, O Lord! O Lord, hear my voice!
Let your ears be attentive to the voice of my pleas for mercy!

—Psalm 130:1–2

The Agony of the Chute

CONSTANCE

ON MY WAY TO RUN errands, I stopped to deposit the garbage down the trash chute of our apartment building. I opened the chute door with my left hand and shoved in the trash bag with my right. In *very slow motion,* I watched my wristlet key chain slide off my arm and down the chute. While, it seemed slow, it was not slow enough for me to grab before it hit the bottom of the compactor!

I was leaving for Israel in three days. I had arranged for Stephanie to fly down to be with her dad while he was still recovering from surgery. Since I was departing during the morning and Stephanie was arriving in the afternoon, I mailed my extra car key to her so she could drive my car home. The problem was, I couldn't drive the car to the airport; the only key I still had went down the trash chute! And I needed all of my keys—car, house, storage room, mail box, etc.

I did everything I could think of to get management to allow me into the compactor to retrieve my keys. I even threatened to slide down the chute myself! I refused to believe they couldn't open it for me. Upset and back in my apartment, I shut my bedroom door, sat on the floor, and cried to God, asking for a miracle. I believed

God could retrieve those keys, but He didn't. After thirty minutes of wailing and praying, I opened the door and said to Carroll, "Well, this is serious, but it's not life or death." It had felt that way an hour before but no longer.

My humbling lament before God, as David often exemplified in his psalms, drove me to surrender everything to the Lord. Emptying my heart and soul, asking for mercy, was the impetus to bringing me peace that morning. My attempts to artfully figure out a plan to accommodate Carroll's needs, have a car available at the airport for Stephanie, and retrieve the lost keys were gone. Christ was who I had. He was all I needed to bring life, breath, and peace back into focus. We always have a choice—let emotions rule or bring Jesus into our messy lives to sort it out.

You know the answer! Jesus is our Friend, the Holy Spirit is our Comforter, and the Father is our Dad. Knowing deep in our hearts that God is with us is comforting to our souls, and that comfort is always available to you in Jesus.

The Privilege of Prayer

NIKI

IN TRAGIC CIRCUMSTANCES not long ago, Joe and I sat together on the edge of our bed, knees gently touching. My hands were tightly clasped in his as tears ran rivers down both of our faces. We didn't know what else to do but cry out our anguish to God. Our prayers came from the depths of our spirits, sometimes not even using words. It's impossible for me to believe God wasn't bending down to listen to our desperate pleas. Have you ever found yourself in that anguished place? Where all that's possible is crying out to the Lord?

It's in our times of despair that our hearts pray earnestly. I poured my whole self into my prayer that dark night. I've since had time to ponder it, though. Why does it take something brutally hard to pray with all that I am? Shouldn't my every prayer be prayed that same way?

Our brains are wired to seek out routine, habit, the path of least resistance. It's through routine we're able to function without much thought to what we're doing. While that may be a good thing while scrubbing a toilet, it's dangerous when it comes to our prayer life. Prayer can become so familiar we may find ourselves saying words that over time can become meaningless. We forget we're actually communing with the Creator of the universe. We say the same words we said yesterday and the day before and the day before that. Surely, it must break God's heart when we forget we're talking to Him and utter rote prayers.

The author of Psalm 130 knew despair, and it brought him to pray fervently for God's mercy. Mercy is about God's kindness and compassion, about how He forgives us when we repent and return to Him, instead of punishing us for our sin. There is nothing so desperate as to be separated from God. The psalmist knew it, and it brought him to pray for reconciliation. He knew the God to whom he prayed, and he was focused on God when he penned these words.

Take a minute to read Revelation 4. John uses the best words he knows to describe the God to whom we speak when we pray. No matter what our situation—joy or despair or something in between—let's remember what a privilege God gave us through Jesus Christ to come before His throne and speak from our hearts. Though we desire to pray ceaselessly, we never desire our prayer to become routine. Let's take a moment every time we pray to remind ourselves of the God of Revelation 4. May we always pray from the depths of our spirit because we know the God who is listening.

Dearest God, I surrender my fears, hurts, and needs to You today.
Bring my focus to who You are every time I come into Your presence
in prayer. Thank You for Your gift of peace. You are my King! Amen.

Day 72

*"Behold, I stand at the door and knock. If anyone
hears my voice and opens the door, I will come in
to him and eat with him, and he with me."*

—*Revelation 3:20*

Knock, Knock

NIKI

MY GRANDKIDS LOVE KNOCK-KNOCK jokes. The goofier the better!
The best ones either make you groan, chuckle, or chuckle while you
groan. Here's a groaner to enjoy.

Knock, knock.
Who's there?
Hal.
Hal who?
Hal will you know if you don't open the door?

In every knock-knock joke, the joke comes in not knowing who
stands at the door knocking, and then in seeing the obvious irony of
the answer.

In Revelation 3:20, though, Jesus plainly tells the world that
it's He who is knocking. Keep in mind, this letter was written to a
believing church. The church in Laodicea was lackadaisical, neither
having enthusiasm nor determination. Their faith was a lazy faith.
This verse, in particular, speaks to the individual believer ("anyone") in

242

that church. It holds a beautiful promise for believers ("I will come in to him"), no matter the state of their faith. It's so indicative of God's love, grace, and mercy.

God pursues us, not only to bring us to faith in Him, but also to bring us back to Him when our faith is weak. So, what might Christ's knocking look like when He's trying to get our attention, and what does He offer when we hear and respond to His knock?

Often, Christ's knocking takes the form of the circumstances He allows into our lives, especially when difficult. When we come to the end of ourselves because of a hard situation beyond our control, we're more likely to turn to Jesus. God often uses suffering to open our ears and our hearts. When we're able to contemplate what God desires, we can learn from our suffering. It's then that we're able to hear God's voice and invite Him in. God doesn't owe us any explanation for why He allows anything. To be clear though, He doesn't waste any circumstance, painful or joyful.

God's response to our inviting Him into our circumstances is such a beautiful word picture. He comes in to us, eats with us, and we with Him. In other words, He abides with us. One definition of abide is "to accept without objection." That's what God does for us. He accepts us despite knowing our hearts and our propensity to wander. He never turns His back but will knock again and again. Let's keep our ears open to hear it, recognize it, and respond.

The Invitation to Feast

CONSTANCE

THIS SCRIPTURE BRINGS ME GREAT joy because it fills me with wonder. Imagine Jesus knocking at your door, desiring to come in and share a meal with you! He's hoping we open the door and welcome Him into our hearts.

In preparation for dinner guests, I ready my home and prepare our meal. I'm filled with expectation as I wait for that knock on the door indicating my guests have arrived. The evening begins, and I settle in for a wonderful conversation over a candlelit meal and some wine. The atmosphere is filled with joy, laughter, and storytelling. We grow a little closer to each other after that knock on the door.

In a way, a meal with friends is a simplification of the way we approach the communion table at church services. The bread is blessed, broken, and given to us as we participate together in celebration of Jesus' body and blood poured out for us. As I return to my seat, I contemplate the beautiful event celebrated together by the family of God all over the world.

Much of Jesus' ministry involved feasting, sometimes at a table and other times around a fire along the shore or reclining and dining with others. Jesus wants intimacy with us, and oftentimes, intimacy occurs when we gather together for a meal. Jesus modeled it beautifully.

In John 21:1–12, Jesus appeared on the beach at the Sea of Tiberias after His resurrection. Upon seeing His disciples fishing, He invited them to bring some of the fish they had caught and have breakfast. Jesus served them bread and fish, and suddenly, His disciples recognized Him as the Lord. It was not only breakfast but also a time shared together with Jesus.

What is the mystical thing that happens when we sit with Jesus alone in the morning? The quietness creates a posture that attunes us to hearing God's voice more clearly than the thoughts swirling in our heads. We hear the knock, the nudge, and the still, small voice. We open the door to our hearts and recognize Him, the Bread of Life, inviting us to communion together. We meet Him with eyes opened and knowledge of who He is. How will you respond to His knock this day?

Jesus, may I always answer when You knock. Thank You for never giving up on me, no matter how far I wander. Amen.

Day 73

*. . . a time to tear, and a time to sew; a time to
keep silence, and a time to speak . . . .*
—Ecclesiastes 3:7

The Song

CONSTANCE

SITTING TOGETHER AT THE KITCHEN island, Sebastian and I
tapped our feet to his favorite song, "Fishing" by Widespread Panic,
one he has loved for twenty-two years. I wondered why this is still
his favorite. We listened to the words that mean so much to him.
When his song ended, I shared one of my favorite songs from the
Avett Brothers, "No Hard Feelings." We sat together in silence,
listening to music that mattered to both of us for reasons we each
held tightly. This endearing moment, listening to each other's heart
longings through song, is a memory I treasure. The deep feelings in
him became immersed in the present with me.

Jesus initiated conversations with people throughout the Gospel
writings. One interesting encounter was with Zacchaeus, a wealthy
tax collector, who was up in a tree along the road, waiting for Jesus
to pass on a particular day. As Jesus walked by, He looked up and saw
Zacchaeus. He called to him to hurry down from the tree and then
invited Himself to Zacchaeus' home.

I can only imagine what an evening with Jesus might look like!
Maybe a meal was in order, likely with captivating conversation.

Zacchaeus might have been anxious to engage Jesus about the stories he had heard of Him. Was He the miracle worker, the teacher of strange words, the coming Messiah others said He was? Zacchaeus might have had some things to share about his life, too. I expect there were moments of deep spirit connection between them. Jesus ends the day with, "Today salvation has come to this house . . . . For the Son of Man came to seek and to save the lost" (Luke 19:9–10). Zacchaeus' life was changed by the Presence of Jesus.

There are no limitations to the ways of experiencing something special with another, a moment in time—seeing a son through his favorite song, walking in silence with someone through a garden, having coffee and a biscuit with a friend. It's all beautiful and meaningful.

Invite Jesus to your quiet place, then wait for Him to speak.

Joyful Mourning

NIKI

IN THE LAST SIX YEARS, I'VE HAD two sisters-in-law (N and J) pass away. N, who died suddenly, didn't know Jesus. I realize we're not privy to knowing someone else's heart, but the way she lived looked far away from knowing and loving the Lord. I felt a darkness descend over my own heart at her passing because there was no longer any opportunity for her to surrender her life to our Savior. I still grieve the state of her eternity and hold sorrow at not having tried harder to help her see and experience how much God loved her. I squandered the time I had to speak and instead gave up, keeping silent because I knew she didn't want to hear me.

J passed away two years ago. She did love the Lord, and what a difference that makes in mourning the loss of this woman I loved.

She was diagnosed with terminal cancer four years before her death. When she passed, everyone who knew and loved her celebrated her life and the truth that she was face to face with our Lord and Savior. What a party must have been happening in heaven to welcome her home! We were sad but joyful at the same time.

In biblical times, when Solomon penned Ecclesiastes, a common sign of mourning was to tear one's clothes. Without having to say a word, the torn clothing let others know you'd suffered a loss and were grieving for a loved one. But with the passing of my sisters-in-law, I realized there are two different states of mourning. The grief for one who is likely lost is never-ending. The grief for one whom we can be confident is with our Lord is tinged with joy even as we grieve. We can "sew" up our grief with joy and, eventually, think more of the celebration and rejoicing that our loved one is experiencing in God's presence. God knows we'll grieve, but our grief can't help but give way to the joy of our loved one reaching the prize we're all longing for.

All time is held in God's hands. The time of our birth and the time of our death. Our time to speak the truth of Jesus is now—while we still have breath in our own bodies. Think of someone you love who doesn't know Jesus. There's no time to wait.

Loving Father, thank You for the many ways You show me how to commune with you. Give me the courage I need to share Jesus with someone who doesn't know You. Amen.

Day 74

And as they were stoning Stephen, he called out, "Lord Jesus, receive my spirit." And falling to his knees he cried out with a loud voice, "Lord, do not hold this against them." And when he had said this, he fell asleep.

—*Acts 7:59–60*

As the World Watched . . .

NIKI

ON JUNE 17, 2015, TWENTY-ONE-YEAR-OLD Dylann Roof walked into Mother Emanuel A.M.E. Church in Charleston, South Carolina. He was welcomed into a Bible study, but a short time later, he shot ten people in attendance, killing nine and injuring one. Two days later, at his first court appearance, one by one, relatives of the victims stood and said to Dylann, "I forgive you," as the nation called for justice.

The country watched as grieving family members offered Dylann forgiveness instead of crying out for vengeance in that courtroom. I remember watching the newscasts and witnessing the shocked reaction of the broadcasters. The nation's attention was turned to the Lord that day. God was glorified on national television! It was an incredible moment to witness, and it moved my lips to praise God even amidst my sorrow.

The mercy of those families is not natural to the human heart. It can only be offered from a heart submitted to Jesus. Two thousand years ago, the same kind of heart was displayed in Stephen, who asked

God to forgive his murderers even as they were stoning him. Stephen's words echoed those of Jesus on the cross when He asked His Father to forgive those crucifying Him before breathing His final breath.

In all three cases—the Charleston families, Stephen, and Jesus—the ability to forgive comes from a place of knowing who the true enemy is. Not people, but Satan. "For we do not wrestle against flesh and blood, but against the rulers, against the authorities, against the cosmic powers over this present darkness, against the spiritual forces of evil in the heavenly places" (Ephesians 6:12). I've held this verse in my mind and close to my heart in times when I've experienced evil in my own life. Remembering who the enemy is, who I'm truly up against, is the only way I've been able to forgive the people who have perpetrated evil against me or my family.

God misses nothing, and vengeance is His. He will repay (Hebrews 10:30). God's command to me is to love (enemies and all) and to forgive. Both are possible through the supernatural power of the Holy Spirit within the hearts of those given over to Jesus.

Forgiveness Is Freedom

CONSTANCE

MY SISTER AND I HAVE STRUGGLED with our relationship for most of our lives. Many times, hurtful things were said that required separation and boundaries. I knew the "godly" thing was to forgive. I did utter those words, but the hurt and anger remained. I wrestled with finding words to pray for her, so I asked God to love my sister through me. In my quiet time with God, I began to notice the Spirit ushering me into her sadness and grief. I recognized her struggles and hurt, remnants of our childhood, and began to experience compassion

250

for her. As God allowed me to see her brokenness and need for love, my feelings of anguish and anger slowly evaporated. A blanket of love and healing covered me. Day by day, our relationship continues to bloom with kindness and love.

Stephen's endurance through stoning until his death gives me pause. Hated, abused, and misunderstood, Stephen called out with a loud voice before surrendering his spirit to Jesus, "Lord, do not hold this sin against them." Can you imagine? Stephen, in ultimate humility and love, surrendered his need for God's just punishment for the sin that caused his death.

I wonder what those around Stephen felt in that moment. Were their hearts pierced with painful regret or still holding on to their anger against him? I imagine most of us won't face what Stephen did; however, we likely have been "stoned" by the words of others that are difficult to forgive. But forgiveness doesn't mean forgetting; instead, it takes away our need for retribution. It gives freedom and peace.

In the midst of an atmosphere where others were filled with rage, Stephen was "full of the Holy Spirit, gazed into heaven and saw the glory of God, and Jesus standing at the right hand of God" (Acts 7:55). The power of the Holy Spirit gives us the ability to forgive and display love instead of hatred. When you invite God to love others through you, as I did with my sister, the Spirit allows us to see the deeper heart pain they're holding. We may be unaware of underlying triggers from our painful pasts that drive us to respond to others in inappropriate ways. God does see and desires to heal these places in our hearts. Cherish this treasured gift.

Father, help me to forgive with compassion. I understand my own need for forgiveness. Offering it to others is one of the most divine works I can do. Amen.

Day 75

I am continually with you; you hold my right hand. You guide me with your counsel, and afterward you will receive me to glory. Whom have I in heaven but you? And there is nothing on earth that I desire beside you. My flesh and my heart may fail, but God is the strength of my heart and my portion forever.

—Psalm 73:23–26

Longing for Contentment

CONSTANCE

THERE IS LITTLE DOUBT THE WORLD has suffered greatly these past few years. In our connected humanity, we see the world as more divisive, less safe, and more uncertain about the future. My heart feels this ever-changing mess of a world and the trauma it holds. The temporary comfort of filling our days with activities leaves us feeling tired, numb, and empty. How are we to navigate such a world? I know what I want and need and so does God—a kinder world.

The psalmist knew the remedy for an ailing heart comes in loving God. Does the Creator of the universe hold a place in your heart more captivating than anything else in your life? If everything you have disappeared today, could you say, "God is the strength of my heart and my portion forever?" Our longings for love, joy, peace, and kindness are satisfied by an intimate relationship with God. He is our destiny. In loving Him, we have all we truly need.

We can stand strong through the difficult days ahead with confidence in God. We are strengthened with power through His Spirit in our inner being, grounded in love, and filled with all the fullness of God in spirit, soul, and body.

We may ask ourselves, *Can I trust you, Lord, to guide me and sustain me through life?* Yes, not only can we trust Him, but Jesus will also supply the peace we need even when everything around us seems to be falling apart. Remember, fallen world conditions were a reoccurring story throughout the Bible. Though they look different for our generation, the remedy is the same as it was in ancient times. Let's place our hope and trust in the Almighty God, worship and praise His glorious name, recognize our strength comes from Him, and know His steadfast love endures forever.

Unlimited Joy Forevermore

NIKI

ASAPH BEGAN THIS PSALM LAMENTING the good fortune of the wicked. He saw wicked people prospering, causing him to wonder about the justice of God. But here in these later verses, he has a change of heart. He reminds himself God is trustworthy, faithful, and just. Asaph remembers it's not his place to compare how God deals with someone else with how God deals with him. It's the same for us.

God's blessings and resources are infinite. He'll never run out, no matter how much He gives to someone else, wicked or otherwise. Someone else's blessings have nothing to do with us and our relationship with God.

Have you ever traveled to a poverty-stricken country? What you may notice is that believers who have very little in material blessings and resources have an abundance of joy. Their love for the Lord spontaneously spills out of them. Why is that so? I think it's possible they understand the same thing Asaph came to understand. God is the source of all joy!

I witnessed that kind of joy years ago while in Togo, Africa, on a medical mission trip. As we walked through a local village, a woman invited us into her home. She had such joy in her hospitality. It didn't matter that her home, where she cared for several children, was a one-room hut with a dirt floor and no furniture, only hammocks for sleeping. Cooking was done outside over a fire. But, she knew Jesus, and so she had joy! Even in the face of hardship, our source of joy can never be taken from us. An intimate relationship with the Lord comes to mean more than anything the world has to offer.

"Whom have I in heaven but you?" What a great question. If God weren't in heaven, why would we ever want to go there? He is the source of everything good, of all joy. He is the Light of the World, the Bread of Life. He is love unfathomable. Open your heart and ask Him to pour Himself in. Nothing will fill you like God will fill you—here and now and for all of eternity with Him in heaven.

Father, Jesus, Holy Spirit, help me to feel Your
presence in my life each day. Amen.

Day 76

Where there are no oxen, the manger is clean, but
abundant crops come by the strength of the ox.

—Proverbs 14:4

The Harvest Can Be Messy

NIKI

IT'S TIME FOR TRUE CONFESSIONS. My self-protection modus operandi is withdrawal and even isolation if necessary. On top of that, I'm an introvert to the extreme. I'm also a homebody. No place I'd rather be than home. Exciting life, yes?

I know all of these things about myself, and yet I desire to live a fruitful life, bearing an abundant harvest for the Lord. And so, I know I have to step outside my comfort zone and into the "messiness" and interruptions of people.

Jesus modeled a life of stepping into the messiness of others. He sought out the sinful and even dined with them. He entered the homes of the diseased and got his hands dirty in healing the sick and the blind. He had compassion for society's outcasts and the condemned. Jesus came to seek and save the lost, not to keep his "manger clean."

Jesus was also open to interruption. He never turned anyone away because He was too tired, too hungry, too busy, or too stressed. But even in His perfect life of love and service, He needed to get away from others to be alone with His Father. It's in those times He was replenished and filled with all He needed to step back into the messiness and interruptions of people. As a Man intent on accomplishing His Father's mission, Jesus needed to be refilled and recharged, and so do we. The way Jesus was replenished by time alone with the Father leads me to believe He just might have been an introvert, too. Yet, through His death and resurrection, following the Father's will, His harvest is all of humanity.

If we, as Christ-followers, desire to live a life like He did, accomplishing the mission and reaping a harvest, we have to be willing to step into the lives of others, messiness and all. Paul understood the model of Christ's life and encouraged the early church (and us) to understand and emulate it: "Let each of you look not only to his own interests, but also to the interests of others. Have this mind among yourselves, which is yours in Christ Jesus" (Philippians 2:4–5). Withdrawal and isolation have no place on the fields of abundant harvest.

Strong as an Ox

CONSTANCE

IN PONDERING OUR KEY VERSE, God whispered to my spirit, *You are the ox!* Surprised and curious, I dug deeper into learning about these plant-eating, oversized animals. Oxen actually have a calm temperament and a willingness to respond to commands when an extra bit of muscle is needed for the job. With their stature and strength, oxen have been used by farming communities throughout the world for over six thousand years. They aren't the most cuddly or cutest animals around, but they have emotional stamina to endure the challenges presented to them.

I imagine most of us have experienced what is sometimes referred to as "the dark night of the soul." These are times of deep pain that can wear us down. For some of us, it feels like we're hanging on by our fingernails, and one more thing or word would drop us into total darkness. But we don't let go, even as the battle rages. Satan's intent is to get us to deny God when we're truly desperate.

Then suddenly, we see the light in the darkness. The destructive force of the enemy didn't win, and we realize *we're strong like an ox*. My fellow survivors, we may be walking with a limp, but we're stronger despite our weaknesses. Our strength is God's strength in us. Our willingness to press in while we are in the darkest valley brings joy to our Father.

Like the ox, we willingly submit to God's commands and find our empowerment in Him. Our emotional stamina, temperament, and endurance through the dark night provide abundant fruits of faith, steadfastness, long-suffering, goodness, wisdom, and much more. The beauty comes in freely sharing those fruits with others facing their own dark nights.

God's Word always has something good for us. When we're seeking to better know Him and are willing to wait for His response, the Holy Spirit will bring clarity through the Word. Perhaps it's direction or instruction, sometimes correction or comfort, but definitely enlightenment on the character of God.

Dearest Father, help me to step outside my place of comfort and into the lives of others. May I lean on Your strength when I am weak. Amen.

Day 77

*Search me, O God, and know my heart! Try me and
know my thoughts! And see if there be any grievous
way in me, and lead me in the way everlasting!*

—Psalm 139:23–24

Praise, Lament, Examination

CONSTANCE

PSALM 139 IS ONE OF MY FAVORITES. Not only is it a beautiful,
poetic prayer of adoration to God, but it also includes David's emotional honesty and knowledge of evil that ultimately leads him to
invite God to search and examine his heart.

David knew the wonder and mystery of God's love for him. Not
only did God know David's every word and thought, but God also
knew him before he was conceived. There wasn't a place he could go
where God wasn't with him. The close relationship we see between
God and David is beautiful: man recognizing the enormous depth
of the love of the Creator of the universe.

But then something happened. David's poetic praise rolled into
rage for those who spoke malicious intent against his beloved God.
His heart was filled with hatred and passion for retribution. The seed
of hate and bitterness toward those who have done us wrong slowly
infects our hearts, souls, and bodies in destructive ways. We soon find
ourselves sounding like the despicable evil we hate. We're angry and
want those who have caused our pain to pay.

David's praise turned to lament, but then he asked God to search his heart and lead him in the everlasting way—the way bringing life for him and praise for God. At times, God needs to examine our thoughts and reveal the grievousness in our hearts. May we cry out to Him and pray, "Create a clean heart and right spirit within me." We then can return to His path where we hear His voice and know His ways.

Do I Really Want to Know?

NIKI

IN ALL HONESTY, THESE TWO VERSES give me a bit of anxiety. David penned them at the end of his psalm praising God for how well He knows everything about David. He knows his thoughts; He knows when he sits or stands; He even knows all the inner workings of his body because He created David. Why then is David asking God to search him and know his heart and his thoughts? The searching is not for God's benefit but for David's.

Why the anxiety in asking God to search and know *my* heart and thoughts? Just like for David, God already knows. What makes me anxious is that *I* don't really want to know! The New Living Translation of verse 24 says, "Point out anything in me that offends you . . . ." What offends God? Sin. If I ask God to point out any hidden sin He finds in me, then I'll need to face it, admit it, confess it, and repent of it.

While I know God offers mercy, grace, forgiveness, and nothing but love, my prideful heart can resist looking for hidden sin. Blatant sin is one thing; hidden sin that I don't recognize as sin, or maybe want to hide even from myself, is another. Yet, I know there is freedom in confessing and repenting, in being forgiven with boundless, unconditional love. *I do* and *I don't* want to know all that is in me that offends God. I want to be forgiven and change my ways, but I don't want to face what it might mean about my heart right now and what I may need to do about it. Sweet friend, have you experienced that same ambivalence yourself?

If we're going to be prepared for God to lead us in His way everlasting, then we first need Him to open our eyes fully. Search us, O God, and, *yes,* do show us what offends You.

Father God, give me courage and strength to face all of my sin.
Search my heart and lead me in the everlasting way. Amen.

Day 78

*And let us consider how to stir up one another to love
and good works, not neglecting to meet together, as is
the habit of some, but encouraging one another, and
all the more as you see the Day drawing near.*

—Hebrews 10:24–25

How Can I Help?

NIKI

HAVE YOU EVER SAID SOMETHING to someone that you regret saying? I'm raising my hand! It's often in the form of bringing her down a notch, making her feel small because that's the way I feel. My tongue can sometimes bite. I always regret that kind of behavior because God made us for relationship, and my part in any relationship should always be to encourage, affirm, and build up, not tear down.

Words matter. It's not only the effects of our words that make them matter. Our words are a direct reflection of the condition of our hearts. Jesus said, "What comes out of the mouth proceeds from the heart . . ." (Matthew 15:18). The connection between heart and mouth doesn't get much clearer than that.

So, what's going on in my heart when my mouth speaks words that tear down instead of build up? It's in those moments I forget I'm a daughter of the King. In those moments, I'm finding my identity somewhere other than Jesus.

On the other hand, when I'm secure in my identity as being made in God's image and loved unconditionally by my Savior, then His love will flow from my heart and through my lips to be an encouragement to those around me. That kind of love-centered heart requires ongoing heart surrender to Jesus every moment of every day. God empowers us to overcome discouraging thoughts and speak encouragement as He transforms our hearts. "Don't copy the behavior and customs of this world, but let God transform you into a new person by changing the way you think. Then you will learn to know God's will for you, which is good and pleasing and perfect" (Romans 12:2 NLT).

Love Through Sacrifice

CONSTANCE

ONE OF LIFE'S GREATEST JOYS is being with friends. Experiencing life with brothers and sisters in Christ is imperative in today's culture. We're longing for face-to-face connection as we navigate a digital world. Recent years have fostered a society of lonely people in our neighborhoods and even in our churches. Our hearts need healing, and our bodies need hugs.

The early church of Christ met regularly to encourage and inspire each other in their faith, as they forged forward with Jesus' mission, preaching the gospel throughout the world. In the midst of persecution, there was an urgent need to ensure the family of God would not disperse or lose faith. But still, the writer of Hebrews noticed that some had a lackadaisical approach to meeting together and urged them to not give up. Empathy and harmony were quintessential in the body of Christ then and are still important today.

When believers gather together, we commemorate the Lord's body and blood. We sing psalms of praise and hear the Word spoken into our hearts. We are the body of Christ, and the body needs every member to coexist as God desires. Believers functioning as Jesus modeled with his disciples—supporting each other through prayer and providing for each other's needs—is life-sustaining.

Whether Jesus' return is imminent or far into the future, the world's culture harbors a need for deeper and kinder relationships with one another and with God. In my own church, I witness this searching for a deeper connection with Jesus, as we share meals and our stories together regularly. The benefits of a harmonious, caring community require sacrifice of our time and a willingness to be vulnerable with the deep feelings of our hearts. But sacrifice leads to love, and love is who God is.

As we navigate the trickiness of stepping out of our self-protection and into a more intentional and vulnerable relationship with others, let's trust God to lead us, protect us, and show us the amazing beauty of relational closeness, stirring one another to love and good works.

Holy God, be at work in my heart, moment by moment, that my words may always build others up, encourage them, and honor You. Amen.

Day 79

But the angel said to him, "Do not be afraid, Zechariah,
for your prayer has been heard, and your wife Elizabeth
will bear you a son, and you shall call his name John."

—Luke 1:13

Nine Months of Silence

CONSTANCE

ONE ASPECT OF PRAYER IS REQUESTING God to move in a particular situation on our behalf. We anticipate answers, but sometimes they don't come for a long time. The waiting can make us weary, especially if we're looking for clarity on an issue or resolution for something dear to our hearts.

Scripture tells us Elizabeth and Zechariah were exemplary servants of God, righteous and blameless. I imagine they prayed to have a child for years, but with advancing age, their desire seemed lost. In the midst of this disappointment, the angel Gabriel appears. His appearance troubled Zechariah, and fear overcame him. However, the angel proclaimed that Zechariah's prayer had been answered. He and Elizabeth would have a child named John. Seemingly perplexed, Zechariah questioned Gabriel. The angel answered, "I stand in the presence of God, and I was sent to speak to you and to bring you this good news" (Luke 3:19). Because of Zechariah's unbelief, he was unable to speak for nine months.

Was the silence punishment, as many believe, or was it a gift?

Could this time of silence be preparation for what was ahead for his son John the Baptist and the people of Israel? Is this silence a rest in God's presence for Zechariah?

For Elizabeth, the anticipation and joy to be carrying the forerunner to the Messiah must have been extraordinary. It could also have been a time of reflection for both Elizabeth and Zechariah.

At last, Elizabeth gives birth. Zechariah speaks after months of silence. Can you imagine the words of blessing and thanksgiving poured forth to God as they celebrated the miracle in their lives?

Don't give up on prayer in the midst of apparent disappointment. When our prayers seem lost in the silence, God just might be working on an answer that is larger than the request, and it will come in His timing. May we utilize the time of waiting to recalibrate our hearts and minds to the will of God. Sit with the silence, listening for the Holy One to speak.

Precious, Persistent Prayer

NIKI

MY ELDEST SON DOESN'T KNOW Jesus in a way that changes everything for him. It's the heaviest burden I carry. For years, I've persistently prayed for him to see Jesus for who He is and to surrender his life to Him. If you've ever prayed persistently for someone and have yet to see God move, you know exactly what I'm talking about.

Zechariah and Elizabeth were both advanced in years and still without children. Although it had to be heavy on their hearts, I would guess they would have given up praying about it by that time. Yet, the angel tells Zechariah his prayer has been heard! Can you imagine?

God is about to answer a persistent prayer Zechariah likely prayed for years and had all but given up on. God had heard.

Persistent prayer is part of our relationship with God. It says in 1 Thessalonians 5:1 to "pray without ceasing." James 5:16 says, "The prayer of a righteous person has great power as it is working." But why does God want us to pray when He already knows what we'll ask and how and when He'll answer? When we pray, we focus on God and recognize our dependence on Him. Prayer draws us closer to Him. While God's most frequent communication with us is through Scripture, ours with Him is through prayer. It's the two-way communion of sacred conversation.

While there are many verses in Scripture about prayer, one of the most visually powerful is Revelation 5:8: "And when he had taken the scroll, the four living creatures and the twenty-four elders fell down before the Lamb, each holding a harp, and golden bowls full of incense, which are the prayers of the saints." Our prayers are so important to God that He keeps every single one of them! Those golden bowls full of incense are our prayers, never ignored and never forgotten.

Praying for something over a long period of time, like Zechariah did, and like I do for my son, teaches us to be patient and to trust in God's timing. If God answered every prayer the moment we prayed, we would come to love the gifts more than we love the Giver. Friend, God hears you. You and your prayers are precious to Him. If He hasn't answered yet, keep praying!

Heavenly Father, thank You for hearing my prayers
and answering when the time is right.
I trust in You, Lord. Amen.

Day 80

And they glorified God because of me.

—Galatians 1:24

Glory to God in the Highest

NIKI

I'VE REACHED THE POINT IN MY LIFE where I'm beginning to contemplate leaving some of my possessions to particular people after my death. It's not morbid; it feels like natural planning. My planning has generated some interesting conversations with my kiddos and kiddos-in-law. There are only a few things of value, but it makes sense to make those decisions now to avoid possible conflicts later. I've seen inheritances cause unexpected division in families, and I don't want that to happen to mine.

There's something even more important than possessions to contemplate as we creep up to the finish line of life—legacy. What will I leave behind for those who come after me? We all want our lives to count for something, to have meaning. Have I acted in line with God's purpose for my life?

I was recently in a Bible study where the question was asked, "What do you want your legacy to be?" As we went around the room, everyone's answers were good.

"I want to be remembered as a good wife and mother."

"I want people to remember me as always being kind."

"I want to be remembered as an encourager."

All are wonderful attributes and beautiful legacies.

But Paul writes in Galatians 1:24, "And they glorified God because of me." He probably didn't write that sentence as something he wanted etched on his tombstone, but what an aspiration it could be for us! Paul wrote that sentence after describing the one hundred eighty-degree change in his life after he encountered Jesus. He went from persecutor of the faith to preacher of the gospel. It was evidence of his heart transformation that caused people to glorify God. This kind of heart change only comes from the Lord and is the ultimate legacy of life—a life so transformed by encountering Jesus, others can't help but give praise and glory to God.

I hope that beyond the valuables listed in my will, the true legacy I leave for my family is one pointing them to God. How we live our lives matters. Like it or not, we will leave some kind of legacy behind. May ours bring praise, honor, and glory to our King.

Standing Strong in Faith

CONSTANCE

WHEN LINDA RETURNED THE BOOK I had loaned to her, it had a handwritten note tucked inside. She wrote, "Constance, I thank you for the hands you placed on a stranger's shoulders so many months ago and for all of your prayers." I was moved by her words, but mostly, I was humbled that God would use me to comfort a hurting woman one Saturday afternoon during communal prayer. Obviously, God can do whatever He wants whenever He wants, but I believe He enjoys our submission to the Spirit's nudging to pray, speak into someone's life, listen, or lay hands on another. To learn what this gesture meant to her was powerful. She was glorifying God for how her life was changing from fear-based to trust-based. She's always loved God but never fully put her trust in Him, because her life of disappointments and loss kept her in pain and fear.

Paul wrote his letter to the Galatian church after his conversion from persecuting to preaching the faith he once tried to destroy. The change in him was so dramatic that those around him couldn't help but glorify God. A persecutor of Christ-followers became a believer, inspiring Jesus' followers, who were perhaps suffering because of their faith. No one is beyond God's reach.

After our encounter during prayer, I continued to see Linda at church and to pray for her. I didn't know what was happening in her life, though, until I received her beautifully written note. I was thrilled to hear what God had done in her life as I responded to His call to lay my hands on her shoulder and pray. Her faith is moving mountains and overcoming fears that trapped her in hopelessness for years. I'm filled with joy and hope for Linda. She, in turn, encouraged me! Her note provided me confirmation in discerning the Spirit's voice. We all can be used by God.

What is God endeavoring to do in you that would bring glory to Him? Is it to stand and believe for a miracle when it seems overwhelming and impossible? To endure hardships for a season? To stand for what is right in the midst of culture doing the opposite? Whatever it is, know God will enable you, equip you, and stand with you. He will be glorified because of you.

Father, thank You for making me an instrument of peace and love. May others see Jesus in me and give You the glory. Amen.

Day 81

For this is the will of God, your sanctification . . . .
—*1 Thessalonians 4:3a*

Union With God

CONSTANCE

MY ROAD TO CHRIST WAS NOT the same as Paul's, but like his, my life seemed to change overnight. My decision to accept Jesus' forgiveness in exchange for my shame and self-contempt resulted in a new way of living from that day forward. The longing for the things that didn't quench my heart's thirst were replaced with a yearning for the things of God. My soul and spirit yielded to this beautiful regeneration within me, and it took me by surprise! God was enlarging my capacity to love Him and others. I wanted to move closer to Jesus and walk in the power of the Holy Spirit instead of gratifying the desires of my flesh. This new walk with Christ focused more on His plans for me than my own. My union with God was being restored.

After I accepted Christ, many things radically changed in my life. But in the years since, the changes have become less noticeable, less dramatic, but still so meaningful. He has changed me ever so slowly over a lifetime. These changes are the evidence of the transformation in our lives as we mature in our faith. We become more like Christ as we come to know more about Him. We're sanctified for God's special purposes as we follow Jesus and listen to the Holy Spirit who dwells within us.

The work of sanctification is ongoing. It is the continual redeeming work of God in us leading to ever-increasing knowledge of Him through His Word. I've found that reading the Scriptures helps me find answers and gives me clarity when I'm confused. His way brings me freedom to be who I'm meant to be—His beloved child, free and full of joy.

Sanctification is God's will for us. Lean into Him, breathe with Him, sit with Him, and learn the ways of the Father. Your life will be changed. More and more, you will have the mind and heart of Jesus. Ask your Father to make you holy as He is holy. God said, "I am the Lord who sanctifies you" (Leviticus 20:8). It's His will for you!

Decisions, Decisions

NIKI

HAVING LIVED ON THE EAST coast of the United States for most of our lives, Joe and I have faced the "Should we go? Or should we stay?" question in the days before an oncoming hurricane many times. I consider myself to be decisive, but with the hurricane question . . . not so much. No one wants to evacuate unless it's absolutely necessary. Sometimes, we've stayed and regretted it; other times, we've evacuated and regretted it. What makes it even tougher is that you can't evaluate the current hurricane on what's happened in the past. Every hurricane is unique. Should we go? Should we stay? Our decision could have serious consequences.

How often, too, do we stress over trying to figure out God's will for our lives? We get hung up on making decisions, big and small, that are "in" His will. It seems to me God is less concerned with our decision-making and most concerned with the state of our hearts.

Here, in this one simple sentence in Thessalonians, God tells us plainly, He desires our sanctification. And what is sanctification? It's the Holy Spirit working in us to transform our hearts to become more like the heart of Jesus.

Whether we go or stay, take this job or that job, matters less than doing whatever we do with love and in a way that honors and glorifies God. We are Christ-followers, and our every decision should look more like Christ's life, the Holiest of Holies.

So, give yourself permission to stop fretting over decisions. Ask God for guidance, but above all, make the decision to live for His glory. That decision is the one that matters. With your heart posture right in God's eyes, other earthlier decisions become less important. Pray and then make your best decision while surrendering to the Holy Spirit within you.

Father, may Your will be done in my life through the continuing gift of sanctification. Help keep my heart posture focused on You. Amen.

Day 82

From Womb to Tomb

NIKI

IN THE SUMMER OF MY sixty-second year, I made the decision to stop coloring my hair. My natural color was a deep brown until my early thirties when little glints of silver began to shimmer amidst the darkness. Thus began more than thirty years of an intimate relationship with hair dye. In 2016, I said, "Enough!" And you know what? I love it. I still have some dark brown but also lots of glistening silver streaks.

That's probably why I love this verse in Isaiah, how He will carry us even to when we are old and gray. It's found in a chapter written as a testimony that God is the one true God. The Babylonians, as they fled from their enemy, had to carry their heavy idols on weary animals. And their idols had no power to save them. Their idols were taken captive with them. But our God is the God who carries and saves. In Psalm 139:13–16, God tells of His love and care for us from before we were born, and here, He declares He still loves and cares for us to the end of our lives. God loves us, cares for us, and carries us from the womb to the tomb.

It's funny how one's perspective can change with time and maturity. As I grew older, I began to notice how my artificial dark brown hair started to look harsh against my skin. Now, with my natural colors shining, I can see how nothing suits me better than God's own choice of color for my hair.

"I have made and I will bear; I will carry and I will save." There is no better lifelong truth from our all-powerful and loving God, no matter what color your hair happens to be. As we follow the Lord, God promises to never forsake us. What comfort and peace comes from trusting fully in His promises all the days of our lives. May we always rest in His capable hands.

Take the Reins, God

CONSTANCE

THE DECISIONS I'VE MADE, MANY not so wise, could have benefited from more insight and a wiser perspective. I was the ultimate controller of my life at the time. Years later, I learned I could actually give the reins over to God instead, and it would benefit me greatly.

When I gave my heart and soul to the Lord, I began to see the mess I'd made of my life. Many of my choices were definitely wrong. I thought they were right at the time, but they weren't. God began to show me His heart and the way He wanted me to live. He revealed to me choices that brought me to my knees, weeping for God's mercy, even though I knew He had forgiven me when I surrendered my life to Him. Seeing the truth of our failed choices from God's perspective is the beginning of healing and sanctification. That process continues as we grow in our walk with the Divine.

Isaiah is confirming we're safe from eternal harm in whatever age we find ourselves. Why would we trust anyone, including ourselves, more than we trust God? Does it make me feel differently knowing

He knows everything about me from the womb of my mama? Sure it does! With His help, my choices and decisions are based on the truth of His Word. He sees it all. When a memory of a sin or wound surfaces from the past, I trust it's for a reason. God draws me to sit and talk with Him about it, oftentimes crying, because His compassion toward me is loving and kind. I am forgiven, and I am free.

In the arms of the One who knows us and loves us as no one else can, we find provision and strength to the very end of our days. Surrender all, including control, to Christ's care. Be present in the present with the Presence of God every day. Allow His wisdom to handle the reins. We are His, now and always.

Glorious Father, thank You for the way You love me—
from before my birth and into eternity. I praise You,
Lord, for the years You've given me. May I always
live to bring You praise, honor, and glory. Amen.

Day 83

But Daniel resolved that he would not defile himself with the king's food, or with the wine that he drank. Therefore he asked the chief of the eunuchs to allow him not to defile himself.

—Daniel 1:8

Deeply Held Beliefs

CONSTANCE

HAVE YOU EVER FOUND YOURSELF in a situation that challenged your deeply held beliefs or made you uncomfortable? What if it came from your boss, a principal or administrator, a friend, or your own government? We believe those setting the rules are doing so for our good, but that isn't always true. Not all but many Israelites lived by the laws God set out for them, including some dietary restrictions. These laws provided health benefits but also gave structure to their lives. Daniel understood the importance of honoring God through obedience to His commandments. His heart's desire was a deep relationship with God.

The king believed his menu of food and wine would keep Daniel and his friends healthy and strong for the mission he had for them. Daniel knew otherwise. The chief eunuch was the one to enforce the king's orders; however, God gave Daniel favor and compassion with the chief of the eunuchs, thus allowing Daniel to eat what would not defile him before God. Daniel honored God, and God provided for him.

The king chose Daniel for a purpose, yet Daniel stood up for what he believed. The end result was that Daniel and his friends were healthier and stronger than those eating the king's food and drink. "God gave them learning and skill in all literature and wisdom, and Daniel had understanding in all visions and dreams . . . . And in every matter of wisdom and understanding about which the king inquired of them, he found them ten times better than all the magicians and enchanters that were in all his kingdom" (Daniel 1:17, 20). That's impressive!

It's uncomfortable at times to tell others what you believe to be true. It has been for me. But uncomfortable interactions stretch us; make us stronger, not weaker; and allow us to be more submitted and committed to doing what is right before the Lord regardless of what others think.

Following God requires commitment, courage to endure difficult times, and hope to believe the best is ahead when you do what is right, honorable, and praiseworthy. Is God the desire of your heart? Will you remain unshakeable in obedience to Him no matter what?

One and Done

NIKI

I'VE SHARED THE STORY OF HOW I decided to break my habit of having two glasses of wine with dinner every evening. For two and a half years, I did not have a drop of any alcohol. Then, I told myself it would be nice to have a glass of wine every now and again. So I did. Within a year, I found myself back where I started, having two glasses of wine with dinner every night.

I wasn't having the wrestling with the Holy Spirit I had the first time, though. I don't know why it was different. Maybe the Holy

Spirit didn't need to convict me. I started paying attention to how I was feeling physically and realized with alcohol came several negative physical consequences. My joints were more painful, my blood pressure was higher, my cholesterol was up, and once my sleep was interrupted, I couldn't fall back to sleep. My body felt sluggish, especially in the evenings.

Daniel resolved ahead of time not to give in to the temptation of the king's food and drink. He knew those things would defile him before the Lord. *He decided* before *he faced the temptation.* The same strategy is a good one for us in overcoming the temptations we face. If we pre-commit (decide in advance) to what we're going to do when faced with a particular situation (temptation), we're much more likely to follow through and stick with our commitment. Deciding in advance actually frees our brains from the stress of deciding in the moment. That's what Daniel did.

It's also what I did when I once again decided to put aside wine and take better care of my body. I'm charged with caring for the body God has given me. "Or do you not know that your body is a temple of the Holy Spirit within you, whom you have from God? You are not your own, for you were bought with a price. So glorify God in your body" (1 Corinthians 6:19). For me personally, that verse is convicting.

There is always wine in our house, as I'm not the only one who lives there, and I'm not trying to put my personal convictions onto anyone else. But if I hadn't decided in advance that I would no longer drink wine, I would be facing a decision every evening. I don't want to live with the stress of making a decision over that temptation every single day. Like Daniel, one and done.

Blessed Father, You hold my heart and give me great joy. I pray I honor You always. Thank You for providing all that I need to withstand and overcome the temptations Satan puts before me. Amen.

Day 84

. . . and to know the love of Christ that surpasses knowledge,
that you may be filled with all the fullness of God.

—Ephesians 3:19

A God-Sized Void

NIKI

HOW IS IT POSSIBLE TO KNOW the love of Christ if it surpasses knowledge? It is possible to understand something, to know it, but it can be difficult to make it your own. There's a difference in *knowing* Christ's love in your head and knowing Christ's love with every fiber of your being because you've given your life to Him. One is superficial; the other is life changing. The "be filled with all the fullness of God" Paul talks about doesn't come from head knowledge. It comes with opening your heart and asking God to pour Himself in—His heart directly into your heart.

Have you ever run hard after something, thinking it will be that *one thing* that finally makes you happy and brings contentment? I have. I've lost count of how many different careers I've pursued throughout my lifetime, believing the next one was what I was meant to do. I've lost track of how many projects I've abandoned when I've realized they weren't going to bring fulfillment. All of us have a void within us we're constantly striving to fill. We want other people to fill us—a spouse, children, friends—or other things—a career, a home, a houseful of toys. But the satisfaction, the contentment, the peace found in those things is fleeting. And sooner or later, people will disappoint. It's in our nature.

Only God can fill the emptiness within us because He created us to be in relationship with Him. It's a God-sized void. The sad thing is, most of us don't recognize it. Until you've invited God in and He fills that void, you likely won't even know it's there. It's only when He's changed everything about and in you that you can see what was missing—joy, peace, unconditional love, limitless grace and mercy, contentment, and satisfaction.

I thank God for his patience in pursuing me until I said yes, for I was one of those who had *no idea* I was missing anything. I wonder if the same could be true of you. There is one thing I know for sure. Experiencing God's love in that way, allowing Him to fill you, is like nothing else. It surpasses knowledge! I so want that for you, too.

The Fullness of God Through Intimacy

CONSTANCE

OVER MY LIFETIME, I HAVE ENJOYED a number of deep friendships. The bond between friends and the unity that comes from being part of the family of God can be hard work, but the joy experienced when you've found a true friend is a wonderful gift. I've found that joy in my friend, Niki. We share personality traits and have similar childhood experiences. We have artistic gifts in common, laugh till our bellies ache, are silly but serious, love mission trips, and deeply care for each other. She is me, and I am her.

Most of us long for relationships that allow us to be ourselves.

They are nourishing, loving, trustworthy, and require vulnerability, which creates intimacy. Celebrating our strengths and overcoming our weaknesses provide for beautiful friendships.

I believe God gives us these special friendships as an example of the relationship He desires to have with us. Is it our hearts' desire to know the love of Christ, to love God the way He desires, and to have the closest, most beautiful relationship possible with Him? Knowledge of God is attainable and good, but to experience the fullness of God, we need something deeper.

Augustine, who was often referred to as a saint, said, "We must empty ourselves of all that fills us, so that we may be filled with what we are empty of." We're created by Love for love. As you worship Him from your heart with adoration, watch and see what happens. As you draw near to Him, He will draw nearer to you.

Seek intimacy through communication, be vulnerable, and trust Him. Thrive on the fullness of God that comes from intentional, intimate times of solitude and stillness with Him. Enjoy His benevolent love for you and remind Jesus why you love Him. The reminder will help you keep focused on Him.

Jesus modeled intimacy with His Father, our Father. He and the Father are one, and Jesus always did the will of the Father. The same relationship can be ours and with it comes the fullness of God in Christ Jesus. The love of God surpasses understanding. As we empty ourselves of the unnecessary, He fills us with the important.

*Father, help me to know You and to love You. Open
my heart and pour Yourself in. Amen.*

Day 85

But he turned and said to Peter, "Get behind me, Satan!
You are a hindrance to me. For you are not setting your
mind on the things of God, but on the things of man."

—*Matthew 16:23*

Distract to Attack

CONSTANCE

SEEING RECENT PHOTOS OF MYSELF highlighting my mature age threw me into a tailspin. I am physically fit from exercising most of my life, but the effects from sun and fun have arrived on my skin. So when I needed a professional photo and couldn't capture one that pleased me, I downloaded an app that made me look forty years younger. Ridiculous! When a friend saw my photo the next morning, she asked, "Are you sure you want to use that photo?" My face was slim, long, and baby smooth, but it wasn't me. Aging is part of living a long life. But, challenged by the way I saw myself, I was a mess!

It's been painful coming to terms with my age, but I have begun reimagining the way I see myself and the way God sees me. He sees our hearts and knows our insecurities. We don't see ourselves as He does. Instead, we listen to our own voices and egos that speak otherwise. Those inner critic voices lead to self-contempt. Many of us carry bodily shame from the stories we hold—stories of beauty and harm and, sometimes, even hate. Our bodies crave care, and our spirits thrive when acquainted with our Creator. The words of God are kind, empowering, affirming, accepting, and compassionate, even when correction is needed. I had neglected to hear God's thoughts toward me. He loves me the way I am, and He loves you the same way.

My counselor advised me with several techniques for facing my insecurities. First, acknowledge the truth: I am older, and I don't have the face of a forty-five-year-old. Next, affirm what is good about myself and the gifts God has given me. Last, set my mind on the things of God, not on the things of man, and affirm the Father's words to me: I am His beloved and His beautiful creation. Jesus told Satan to get behind him, and we should do the same.

The evil one had slithered into my thoughts for a knockdown, but it wasn't a knockout. Satan uses our insecurities to distract to attack. Don't get caught in his lies. Take your thoughts captive! I'm reminded to think on what is true, honorable, just, pure, lovely, commendable, and excellent (Philippians 4:8).

We don't need an app to change who we are. We are beautiful, inside and out, because we are sons and daughters of the King.

Temporary

NIKI

PETER'S STORY IS AN ENCOURAGEMENT as I struggle between sin and repentance or speaking and acting before thinking. If ever there was a person in the Bible who can encourage us by his humanity, it's Peter. In Matthew 16:16–19, Peter claimed that Jesus was the Messiah, and Jesus blessed him with the privilege of building the Church. What a holy moment! But, in Matthew 16:22, Peter reprimands Jesus for talking of His coming death, and Jesus responds by calling Peter Satan and a hindrance to His mission. Talk about a flip-flop!

Peter, again, acted impulsively when he sliced off the ear of the high priest's servant as Jesus was being arrested. Peter made many mistakes, and yet God loved him and used him for His Kingdom work. Peter's story gives me hope that God can and will use me, even though I'm far from perfect.

Recently, I met a girl who had a tattoo of the word "temporary." She said her tattoo helps her keep in mind that this world is not our home and to focus on our permanent home with Jesus. What a great reminder to live with an eternal perspective. As we walk through this temporary world, may our focus be on Jesus.

Then there's Satan. It's hard to imagine what Peter felt when Jesus called him Satan. But what better way for the Lord to make His point. Mindset matters. Satan distracts us and entices us away from our mission. Let's give Satan no opportunity. Peter took Jesus' accusation to heart. Later, in his first letter recorded in Scripture, he warned others to watch out for Satan and his enticing, prowling ways. May we be encouraged by Peter's faithful growth and Christ's love and compassion. Satan doesn't win.

Lord Jesus, thank You for Your love for me even in the face of my mistakes and failures. Forgive me. Help me to keep my focus on You and my mind set on eternity. Amen.

Day 86

But we have this treasure in jars of clay, to show that the surpassing power belongs to God and not to us. We are afflicted in every way, but not crushed; perplexed, but not driven to despair; persecuted, but not forsaken; struck down, but not destroyed . . . .

—*2 Corinthians 4:7–9*

Clay Jars and Porcelain Bowls

NIKI

PAUL COMPARES US TO CLAY JARS that are easily broken. It's in our brokenness that God's power is put on full display as humanity is witness to His healing, His redemption, His carrying us when we're too weak to stand. The world needs to hear our stories, brokenness and all.

Christ makes us new and transformed, but what becomes of the broken pieces? Life can break us in so many painful ways, and often, our first line of defense is denial. We try our best to disguise our cracks and broken pieces.

I'm reminded of Kintsugi. Kintsugi, or golden repair, is the Japanese art of repairing broken pottery or porcelain using a special lacquer mixed with either gold, silver, or platinum. The philosophy behind Kintsugi is to recognize the history of the object and to visibly incorporate the repair into the piece instead of trying to disguise it. The finished piece is usually more beautiful than the original.

With Kintsugi, the repair can't be rushed. Each broken piece must be held steady until the golden lacquer sets and locks it firmly in place.

Only then can you move on to the next piece. Rushing Kintsugi by trying to glue several shards at once will result in the lacquer not holding and the piece falling apart. In the end, the repair will take longer. It's the same way with allowing the Lord to heal our broken pieces. Healing is best accomplished in God's time. Our part is to be willing to lay our brokenness at Jesus' feet.

I own a small, icy green porcelain Kintsugi bowl. It's one of my most treasured possessions. Every time I look at it, I'm reminded of God's power to heal and redeem. It's not always easy to embrace the idea of being beautiful and being broken. But just like my beautiful little bowl, those valuable streaks of gold are a part of my story.

No two pieces of pottery are exactly the same, and neither are we. You are unique, your story is unique, and none of us have been broken in the same way. Just as your broken pieces are unique to you so will be your beautiful golden repair. Trust the Creator to redeem your story, and go share it with the world. No one can tell your story but beautiful you.

The Potter's Clay

CONSTANCE

WHILE CONTEMPLATING THIS VERSE, I thought about the weathering rocks and boulders found on lake bottoms and along rivers and streams. When combined with sediment, over time, they create clay. Molding the clay and baking it in a kiln can produce a beautiful piece of pottery, similar to our life stories of struggle and refining to produce beauty. I recall my feeble attempts in pottery class to mold an elephant that wouldn't explode in the kiln. My elephant turned out to be a flat, skinny, and slightly wavy chunk of clay. I was aghast with my creation, though it did make it through the kiln still standing. I now have it displayed on a table in my home to remind me of the experience. My elephant taught me that what Scripture shows me is true. The human, an earthen vessel, experiences struggles and despair, even some heat, but there is a treasure within each of us.

As jars of clay, human beings are capable of enduring multitudes of trials and never-ending attacks on our souls. The heartaches that befall us are redeemed by the power of God. The process of refining and defining is God sculpting us to the likeness of Christ. It's not easy when in the kiln of life's tough experiences, but it feels and looks differently on the other side—our clay jars are full of the power of God. We are strengthened with greater clarity, more stamina, some re-creation stories, and gems of beauty. We understand, as Paul did, the great treasure we have as believers in Christ.

We may have our own slingshot stories as we take down the giants in our lives, as David did. We come to understand the greater meaning in Isaiah 64:8, "O Lord, you are our Father; we are the clay, and you are our potter; we are all the work of your hand." God is refining, molding, and shaping us into the image of Christ. Our surrender is to the One who formed and knitted us together, who says we are "fearfully and wonderfully made" (Psalm 139:13–14).

Father God, help me to know You more completely and embrace Your work to redeem my story. I lean into You during the good times and, especially, the difficult times. Amen.

Day 87

Not that I am speaking of being in need, for I have learned in whatever situation I am to be content.

—*Philippians 4:11*

Re-story Our Lives

CONSTANCE

I NOTICED A RESTLESSNESS WITHIN my soul, a whirlwind of sorts, feeling unsettled in my current circumstances. Carroll and I moved during the pandemic from our 2,100 square foot home into an apartment half the size. What I imagined would be temporary has taken on a more permanent reality for the past two-plus years. I struggle making sense of the changes I'm still facing. Apartment living has its perks—no responsibility—but home living feels more settled. My routine is different, the space more confined, and lots of neighbors above, beneath, and on both sides of us. *How long will it be like this?* I ponder.

Have you ever found yourself yearning for change or searching for the next best thing? It often takes something really significant to cause us to recognize what is most important and change our attitudes and behaviors. Maybe it's a spiritual awakening or reawakening, something that causes us to recognize the true meaning of our human experience.

Paul had such a day of reckoning. He was a man who appeared to take pleasure in persecuting and killing Christians, but Jesus "re-storied" his life on the road to Damascus. Paul hadn't met Jesus personally while He was alive, but when he did meet Him spiritually, he came to know Him in a deeply personal way. Jesus dramatically changed Paul's life.

Could it be the same for us? After years of life experiences and loss, having enough or being in need, accumulating wealth only to see it vanish in a disaster or divorce, do we finally face the ultimate choice to choose contentment? We may realize our hearts need something more than material possessions and worldly worth. Paul came to know the surpassing worth of knowing Jesus as Lord. It was greater than any loss he endured.

I sometimes waffle from season to season. I start committed and grounded in God, then the things of this world grab my attention, and I'm quickly drowning in "me-ism." Thankfully, God never leaves me there. He pursues me until I see my own waywardness and can re-anchor myself in Him. When one's faith and trust are so completely in Jesus, other things once counted important become less so. When we realize nothing of this world satisfies us fully, may we look for contentment in Jesus.

Have you fallen in love with the Giver of eternal life? Now is the time. He yearns for you, and He loves you. He is where true contentment is found.

Content to Bloom

NIKI

JOE AND I WERE WED THE WEEK before his college graduation. A month later, we were on our way to Quantico, Virginia after he was commissioned a second lieutenant in the U.S. Marine Corps. In the twenty-four years we spent in the Marine Corps, we moved eighteen times! In the years since his Marine Corps retirement in 2000, we've moved a few more.

I've always looked at moving as a new adventure and a fresh start. I loved it, but I didn't always love the new location. I'm not the first one to coin this phrase, but I came to live by it over those years in the Marine Corps—bloom where you're planted! That phrase came to mean the same thing to me that Philippians 4:11 likely meant to Paul. Paul faced seasons of plenty and seasons of want. He faced persecution so horrific he didn't think he'd make it out alive. I'm guessing he faced the highest of highs in preaching Jesus Christ and also the lowest of lows in persecution.

What jumps out at me is the phrase "for I have learned." Paul didn't always know contentment. But as God grew his faith and transformed his heart, he came to know he already had everything he would ever need because he had Jesus. God has already met our greatest needs—forgiveness, reconciliation, and relationship with Him—through the death, burial, and resurrection of His Beloved Son. If God never does another good thing for us, we already have what matters because we have a relationship with Him for all of eternity through Jesus Christ. And what we sometimes forget is eternity begins today.

Like Paul learned to be content in whatever situation, I, too, learned to be content and, yes, even came to appreciate every place we've ever lived. People often asked me if I missed this place or that place where we used to live. I'd always honestly answer no. You see, there was another phrase I came to live by during the years we spent in the Marine Corps. I even painted it on a heart-shaped wooden plaque with a little house painted at the top that I hung in our living room in every house we lived in. That plaque read, "Home Is Where the Marine Corps Sends You."

Though we're no longer in the Marine Corps, I can go anywhere and be content and be at home because Jesus goes with me wherever I go. If you've given your life to Him, He goes with you, too. Be content.

Lord Jesus, thank You for going before me and behind me and all around me wherever I go. Help me to bring Your light and love to the place where You've planted me. Amen.

Day 88

*For everything there is a season, and a time
for every matter under heaven . . . .*

—Ecclesiastes 3:1

Reflections

NIKI

WARM WEATHER CAME EARLY this year, and though it's still spring, the trees have already burst forth with their summer greenery. The change of seasons in nature prompts us to look forward to a change in weather and to look with hope at what good things the new season may bring. Changes of season in our lives, though, may cause us to look back in reflection over the season just ending. That's where I find myself today. Joe is about to retire after a working career of forty-seven years, almost the entire length of our marriage. This monumental change has caused me to pause and reflect.

The first thing I see is God's provision. Through Joe's career, God has given us opportunities to provide for our family, though there have been times of scarcity. In those times I see God's faithfulness. One, in particular, is seared into my memory. We were a young family, and Joe was deployed to Japan, without us for six months. We lived paycheck to paycheck in those days, and one month, no paycheck arrived. Missing even one meant the food in our pantry was dwindling. With Joe on the other side of the world, I had to figure it out for myself. After a bit of panic, I decided to pawn our high school rings! Believe it or not, that provision carried us until the financial department of the Marine Corps figured out the issue.

Years later, Joe was laid off from a civilian job and unemployed for five months. Then God opened the door to a job that allowed him to work remotely after a year. That provision enabled us to move halfway across the country to live near our youngest son and his family, a long-awaited dream, all while still having a good job. An unexpected blessing came through the uncertainty of losing one job only to see God provide something better for us.

As Solomon says, "For everything there is a season," and it's our season now to step aside from the working world and into the world of retirement. Reflecting back on what amounts to our whole adult lives, a peace settles over my heart. I can see clearly how God has cared for us through it all. He is faithful, and He is unchanging. I can look forward to this new season and know, because I've looked back and remembered his provision and faithfulness, that God will care for us in every season.

God's Gift to Man

CONSTANCE

THE WISDOM AND POETIC NATURE of Ecclesiastes is beautiful, thought provoking, and full of folly at times. Solomon knows the choices we have in life and the consequences of those decisions. He speaks of a life of folly—that death comes to us all—so enjoy life. He cautions us to remember God and keep His commandments. For Solomon, there is an underlying rhythm or flow for living. As we examine our own lives, we, too, may see a pattern, a direction to the seasons or decades.

I chuckle at the saying, "cats have nine lives" because I have had many myself! When I look back, the gal I was in each "life season" was different. Some seasons changed me, others corrupted me, some brought clarity or confusion, others were valleys of pain, and some were mountain tops of abundance. All taught me something but were not always beneficial.

When people ask me about my childhood, I mention how that little girl was struggling with some awful things. When I was a young woman, I went through a painful divorce and became a single parent making decisions with limited funds. Or maybe I bring up how I gave up on religion and God, but in the next season found Jesus, and everything changed. Each period I was surrounded by circumstances and challenges that produced a myriad of life-giving opportunities for growth while overcoming difficulties. Those kind of challenges can result in reaching out to God in our darkest moments and finding Jesus—the Way, the Truth, and the Life.

It's clear that change happens to us all, but what brings transformation? We obtain clarity in our beliefs because of wisdom we gain along the way. If we choose to grow in knowledge of the Divine, we often experience the most dramatic transformation. Hate turns to love, relationships are respected, and human community matters. It happened for me. However, God doesn't want us to say, "One and done." He wants to give more light as we walk with Him. In our deepening knowledge of God, we can't possibly stay the same. We're students for a lifetime, growing in wisdom and knowledge. A closer walk with Him is a journey worth taking.

Beloved Father, I give You my whole heart and acknowledge that You are the Sustainer of life, and the Breath I inhale. Thank You for Your care and for Your unfailing love. Amen.

*So even to old age and gray hairs, O God, do not
forsake me, until I proclaim your might to another
generation, your power to those to come.*

—*Psalm 71:18*

Listening to Learn

CONSTANCE

DAVID, FROM SHEPHERD BOY TO WARRIOR man, now in old age, prayed that God would grant him the time to invest in another generation, testifying of God's everlasting goodness and faithfulness before he died. He longed for the opportunity to leave a legacy for others to follow. What a beautiful heart's desire to have as we grow older. Most likely, those of us who are in our senior years have traveled down more dirt roads, endured more challenges, and gained a heart of wisdom. We have a mission in our advanced years to demonstrate to a younger generation the love of God and the generous gift of a relationship with Jesus.

I recently invited a friend's son and daughter, separately, out for a meal before they returned to college and high school. We're fond of each other, and they feel like family. I witnessed in Caleb and Gabbi the amazing love they each have for God. Both are musically gifted and desire to share their God-given gifts with others. We exchanged stories and laughter while sharing a meal together, and it knitted our hearts even closer.

The apostle Paul called both Timothy and Titus "my true child in the faith." Paul invested in them the love of a human father and the love of God. Our faith unites us as family with respect, honor, and love.

There is a need for "listening to learn," endeavoring to understand the unique challenges we each face and the insecurities we have about the future. Though Caleb and Gabbi appear, in many ways, to have a wonderful sense of who God is in their lives, displaying it outwardly to others and to God, we elders, in turn, need to offer our friendship and wisdom, a listening ear, and encourage them along the way. Even though we may be decades apart from those we meet, we may have more in common with each other than you would imagine.

The Power of Testimony

NIKI

IT FEELS SURREAL TO BE APPROACHING the end of writing this devotional. The end somehow seems harder than the beginning. I'm trying to stay focused where I am and not look ahead to the finish line, but it has caused me some angst. Do I have what it takes to actually get there?

Every time I write, I first pray for God's direction and wisdom, for insight into the message I'm hearing from Him. I pray He would put His words into my mind and allow them to flow through my fingertips onto the keyboard and then the page. I ask that those words would honor Him, bring glory to His name, and draw others to Jesus. My heartfelt desire is to proclaim Jesus through writing.

Constance and I don't know who will read our devotional or how God intends to use it. That it would reach the whole of another generation would be wonderful, but even if not, we're both leaving an important legacy of our walk with Jesus for our loved ones. After we're gone, our children, grandchildren, and great grandchildren will have this book into which we've poured our hearts to learn things about us and about our love for Jesus they might never have otherwise known. Testimony is important. Whenever we hear testimony about what Jesus has done in someone's life, we can be certain we're hearing God speak.

So even to old age and gray hairs (of which I have many), God has not forsaken me. He's allowed me to continue to proclaim His might and His power to those to come. He will not forsake you either. Share what Jesus has done for, in, and through you. May our testimonies make Jesus known and bring glory to His name. The world needs to hear your story, too.

Almighty One, may Your Spirit be my truth teller and my stories be life giving to those I meet today. Amen.

Day 90

*Come and hear, all you who fear God, and I
will tell what he has done for my soul.*

—Psalm 66:16

Come and See What He Has Done!

NIKI

I WOULD LIKE TO SHARE WHAT GOD has done for my soul through writing this devotional, and my hopes for you in having read these one hundred eighty devotions.

For me, God has:
- Taught me how to deeply meditate on His Word.
- Attuned my ears to hear and eyes to see His message for me in Scripture.
- Revealed His character to me in new ways.
- Brought back to my memory times when He moved, guided, directed, and protected me.
- More deeply captured my heart with the goodness of His provision.
- Given me opportunity to exercise my gifts for His glory.
- Enriched the love and friendship between Constance and me.

My hope for you through this devotional is to:
- See by example how it's possible to hear God's voice and see His personal message in Scripture.

- Cultivate a desire to spend time alone with God every day.
- Realize your time with the Lord will be unique to you.
- Draw nearer to God and know how much He loves you.
- Experience God for yourself in new ways.
- Come to love the Lord more today than you did yesterday.
- Help you reflect on your own life and see how God has always been present with you.
- Dip your toe into writing your thoughts and reflections from your personal time with God—a sentence or two is all you need.
- Embolden you to share with others in some way what God has done for your soul.

It's difficult to put into words all that God has done for me through the months of reading, meditating, and writing. He's blessed me, challenged me, given me courage to be transparent and vulnerable. It has been a joy to share my heart with you.

I pray God's blessing over you, dear reader, as He lights up your life with wisdom and insight and a desire to be with Him daily in His Word. In full surrender, may you allow Him to lead and guide you wherever He would have you go.

Now It Springs Forth

CONSTANCE

ONE DAY, WHILE LOOKING BACK over the decades of my life, I saw a myriad of experiences flowing endlessly across my mind as in a slide show. Friendships woven together that brought meaning and love to my life, places I was blessed to have lived, painful seasons and joyful ones. I saw them all. My life was full, and I had stories to tell!

Before joining the family of God, my unanswered questions were, "Does my life matter to anyone? What's my purpose?" But after I accepted Christ, I realized God had a place for me in His story, and that my story included Him. Looking back, I can see His presence in every second, even when I hadn't yet given Him my heart. But from the moment I surrendered to Jesus, the purpose for the remainder of my life became crystal clear. I am to conform to the image of Jesus and reveal Him to others.

Our stories illustrate our struggle to become like Jesus, our sometimes resistance to following Him, and our joy in running to Him. The script of life events, portrayed on the screen of our human existence, includes the marvelous wooing of God. Scripture, the divine Word of God, interwoven in our stories, encourages us to seek Him daily.

The two years of writing this book and daily meditating on the Word were not only a lifeline during one of the most trying seasons of my life, but it also provided structure and purpose to my days, intimacy with my Father, and a reconnection with personal stories, allowing me to witness God's presence throughout. I experienced the joy of Niki alongside me, especially during our seasons of suffering while reliving stories of God's goodness throughout our lives. We weathered the challenges in our lives together. We absolutely need Jesus, and a beloved friend is His gift to us.

Examine your life through the lens of God's Word; let it speak uniquely to you. Your story matters! Record in a journal the miraculous and redemptive ways God has moved in your life for your family to read later. Let them hear of God's faithfulness and generosity, His kindness and love toward you through all of your days. What has God done for your soul lately?

Abba Father, my heart is Yours. Lead me, guide me, direct me, and I will follow. Thank You for giving me a story to share with the world. Amen.

Acknowledgements

To our husbands, Carroll and Joe . . .
Thank you for your love, care, support, patience, encouragement, and oh, so much more. You have loved us through it all. Thank you for caring for the home front when we snuck away to work together in person. Our love for you knows no bounds.

To our kids, kids-in-love, and grandchildren . . .
In our eyes, you hung the moon. Thank you for being you! There's nothing else you have to do. We love you more than we have words to describe.

To our faithful friends and church family . . .
Thank you for caring deeply about us and our project. Your love and encouragement so often kept us going when we surely wanted to give up.

To our beta readers, Jim and Mary Ann Krauss, Sherry Stormant, Helen Smith, Diane Teigen . . .
Thank you for reading our very rough first draft and providing priceless feedback.

Jim and Mary Ann, thank you for opening your home to us and providing a beautiful lake view, abundant food, and laughter to nourish us as we worked. We are forever grateful for your hospitality, prayers, and love for us and our book. Never have we felt so cared for. We are forever your NiCo.

To our extraordinary editors, Marney McNall and Sarah Wolf . . .
Your constructive criticism and carefully crafted corrections helped us to hone our craft as writers. Thank you for taking on the task of polishing our words to make them the best they can be.

To our eagle-eyed proofreader, Emerald Barnes . . .
Thank you for working so hard and so
quickly to make our writing shine.

To our Lord and Savior . . .
You placed the dream in our hearts and made it come true.
It's Your story, Lord, and we are grateful to be a part of it.
We're blessed to belong to You and so very thankful.

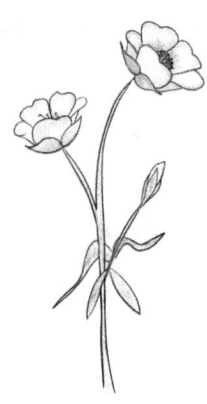

CONSTANCE BROCATO finds delight in the mysteriousness of life and lives with passion and curiosity in her soul. She is an avid reader and loves being outdoors, walking through nature, traveling, mission trips, and contemplative times in solitude and silence each day with the Divine. She thoroughly enjoys engaging others she meets in conversation, oftentimes to hear their stories or provide a listening ear. She believes our stories provide a pathway into healing and a doorway into community.

Her ten years in Hawaii, followed by a twenty-five-year working career in Maryland, led to twelve more years working as a concierge in Charleston, South Carolina. An abundance of life experiences filled forty-five years of journals, which eventually led to writing her first book with Niki Krauss.

She and her husband, Carroll, reside in Mount Pleasant, South Carolina. She's mama to Sebastian, stepmom to Stephanie, mom-in-love to two, and Tutu to three sweet grands. Connect with Constance at constancebrocato@gmail.com.

NIKI KRAUSS is a Yankee by birth, a Southerner by choice, and a joy-filled lover of Jesus by grace. Married to Joe for forty-eight years, Niki is mom to two, mother-in-law to one, and Mimi to three.

During twenty-four years of moving around the country as the wife of a Marine Corps aviator, Niki enjoyed a variety of careers, including exercise instructor, legal secretary, administrative assistant, office manager, and finally, fifteen years as the Assistant Editor for the *Marine Corps Gazette,* the professional journal of the United States Marine Corps, before retiring in 2015. Niki's debut book, *Little Girl Mended: A Memoir,* a recounting of God's healing and redemption of her story of childhood sexual abuse, was published in 2016.

When not writing, Niki enjoys reading, keeping fit, and needlecrafts. Her happy place is her favorite over-stuffed chair near a window, eyes and heart in the Word, journal in hand. Joe and Niki live in Dallas, Texas with their big, old black Lab and their twin gray kitties. Connect with Niki at www.nikikrauss.com, niki@nikikrauss.com.